AF481170

A NOTE FROM THE SUPERINTENDENT

Grace, mercy, and peace to you from God our Father and Jesus Christ our Lord! He that dwelleth in the secret place of the Most High shall abide under the shadow of the Almighty. I will say of the LORD, *He is* my refuge and my fortress: my God; in him will I trust. In many ways, events of this year have caused us sit down under the covering of the Almighty; to stop in his shade, and trust in Him. As we walked through valley of the shadow death, the rod and staff of our shepherd Jesus Christ comforted us. Life changed in many ways, we adjusted to internet Sabbath School and sermons, reflecting on the fellowship we once enjoyed in the sanctuary with the saints. This time has been difficult in many ways for each of us. One thing has not changed, and that is the faithfulness of God. God remains sovereign and in control of everything that occurs in his creation. I encourage you to continue to hold fast to his unchanging Word. Heaven and earth will eventually pass away, but the Word liveth and abideth forever. The primary goal of this compilation of lessons is to speak the Word faithfully and to make it applicable to everyday life. Hopefully, you are able to strengthen your relationship with Jesus Christ through your study of these lessons. Thank you for supporting the Sabbath School; you as members are what make it great! Thank you to every member of the compiling committee for their excellent contributions to this book. Each author is noted at the end of each lesson, except the lessons I authored. Thank you to Apostle G.R. Dailey Jr. and the Apostle Board for their work in compiling this book. If you have any comments or suggestions regarding the lessons, please contact me at: *brohurst@houseofgod.org*

In Christ's Love,
Bro. Joshua Hurst,
National Sabbath School Superintendent

CONTENTS

<u>**On the Cover**</u>: This is a photo of the Orion nebula. It is the closest massive star making factory to Earth, at 1450 light years away! Through his God given dominion, man continues to study and to try to comprehend the heavens that God created in one day!

Amos 5:8 Seek him that maketh the seven stars and Orion, and turneth the shadow of death into the morning, and maketh the day dark with night: that calleth for the waters of the sea, and poureth them out upon the face of the earth: The LORD *is* his name:

Cover layout by Minister David Wallace, Jr.
Cover photo courtesy of NASA.

HOUSE OF GOD Sabbath School Lessons

Holy Church of the Living God

'he Pillar and the Ground of the Truth

The House of Prayer for All People

(PENTECOSTAL)

The Late Bishop R. A. R. Johnson, D.D., M.B., Founder
The Late Bishop A. A. Smith, D.D., Ph.D., first Chief Apostle
The Late Bishop S. P. Rawlings, B.S., Th.D., 2nd Chief Apostle
The Late Bishop F. C. Scott, D.D., 3rd Chief Apostle
The Late Apostle James E. Embry, Jr. 4th Chief Apostle
Apostle Thomas E. Clark, Jr., Chief Apostle

Sabbath School Superintendent: Brother Joshua Hurst
Assistant Superintendent: Minister David Wallace Jr.

Compiling Committee: Brother Joshua Hurst, Evangelist Irene Crawford, Elder James Taylor Jr., Elder David Brand Jr., Evangelist Patricia Powell, Minister Robert O. Johnson

September 2020-September 2021

SABBATH SCHOOL ORDER OF SERVICE

Song by Congregation

Prayer whom he or she may designate

Responsive reading

Superintendent: Let my cry come near before Thee, O LORD give me understanding according to Thy word.

School: Let my supplication come before thee: deliver me according to Thy word.

Superintendent: My Lips shall utter praise when thou hast taught me thy statutes.

School: My tongue shall speak of thy word for all thy commandments are righteousness.

Superintendent: Let thine hand help me; for I have chosen thy precepts.

School: I have longed for thy salvation, O LORD and thy law is my delight.

Superintendent: Let my soul live, and it shall praise thee; and let thy judgments help me.

School: I have kept thy precepts and thy testimonies: for all my ways are before thee.

Superintendent: Teach me, O LORD, the way of thy statutes; and I shall keep it unto the end.

School: Give me understanding, and I shall keep thy law: yea, I shall observe it with my whole heart.

Superintendent: Make me to go in the path of thy commandments; for therein do I delight.

School: Incline my heart unto thy testimonies, and not to covetousness.

Superintendent: Turn away my eyes from beholding vanity; and quicken thou me in thy way.

School: Stablish thy word unto thy servant, who is devoted to thy fear.

Superintendent: Turn away my reproach from which I fear: for thy judgments are good.

School: Behold, I have longed after thy precepts: quicken me in thy righteousness.

Superintendent: Wherewithal shall a young man cleanse his way? By taking heed thereto according to thy word.

School: My son, forget not my law, but let thine heart keep my commandments:

Superintendent: For length of days, and long life, and peace, shall they add to thee.

School: Let not mercy and truth forsake thee: bind them about thy neck; write them upon the table of thine heart.

Superintendent: So shalt thou find favor and good understanding in the sight of God and man.

School: Trust in the LORD with all thy heart; and lean not unto thine own understanding.

All: In all thy ways acknowledge him, and he shall direct thy paths.

Review of the Twenty Four Principles

Classes arranged for study period

Classes report offering

Secretary's report

Lesson review

Receiving of members

Benediction

SABBATH SCHOOL SONG

Words by Elect Lady Mary Campbell, 1109 Prince Street, Beaufort, S.C.
To Be Sung in the Tune Of "We've Come This Far by Faith"
We're members of the Sabbath School, every Sabbath Morning.
This is the way we learn God's word, and all of His
commandments. We need His word to fight the devil, who's
trying to block our way.
So come to Sabbath School, you will meet God there. Please be
on time for your own soul's sake, for Jesus was never late.
Repeat

CHURCH ANTHEM

This is the church of the living God.
The pillar and ground of the truth,
The house of prayer for all people,
Commandment keepers are we.

We do not drink no wine,
We do not eat no swine.
We keep all the sayings of the Lord our God,
Commandment keepers are we.

We keep the Ten Commandments,
We keep the Sabbath too.
We keep all the feasts of the Lord our God,
Commandment keepers are we.

This is the church of the living God.
The pillar and ground of the truth,
The house of prayer for all people,
Commandment keepers are we.

SABBATH SONG

The seventh day is the Sabbath.
The seventh day is the Sabbath.
The seventh day is the Sabbath of the Lord.

The seventh day is the Sabbath.
The seventh day is the Sabbath.
The seventh day is the Sabbath of the Lord.

We do our washing on Sunday,
We do our ironing on Monday,
Tuesday and Wednesday, we work the same.
Clean our house on Thursday,
Shop a half day Friday,
Preparing for the Sabbath of the Lord.

The seventh day is the Sabbath.
The seventh day is the Sabbath.
The seventh day is the Sabbath of the Lord.

The seventh day is the Sabbath.
The seventh day is the Sabbath.
The seventh day is the Sabbath of the Lord.

CONTACT INFORMATION

General Headquarters
866 Georgetown Street
Lexington, KY 40511

Mailing Address
P.O. Box 13010
Lexington, KY 40583

Main Extension   **859-413-2705**

Apostle Thomas E. Clark Jr.   **859-413-2719**

Apostle G. Randolph Dailey Jr.   **859-413-2720**

Apostle James Ragland   **859-413-2728**

General Secretary   **859-413-2732**

General Treasurer   **859-413-2730**

Jamaica Superintendent   **876-865-9271**

Cash App *$house866*

1. **The new birth, ye must be born again:** Jn. 3:1-7; I Jn. 3:9; Acts 2:1-4; II Cor. 5:17.

2. **The keeping of the Ten Commandments written by God's own finger:** Ex. 20:1-17; Ex. 31:18; Ex. 32:15-16; Ecclesiastes 12:13; Jn. 14:15; Rev. 22:14-15.

3. **Divine Healing:** Ex. 15:26; Isa. 53:4-5; Mark 9:23: Jn. 9:6-7.

4. **The administration of feet washing and communion at the same service:** Jn. 13:4-17; Matt. 26:26-27; I Cor. 11:28-29

5. **Tithes and offerings, an early duty of the people of God:** Gen. 28:22; Lev. 27:30-32; Matt. 23:23; Heb. 7:5.

6. **The eating of selective foods as holy people should:** Lev. 11:1-47; Deut. 14:1-21; Isa. 65:4-5, 66:17; Acts 15:20.

7. **Everlasting life before going through the grave:** Hos. 13:14; Jn. 3:16; I Cor. 15:51; Jn. 8:51.

8. **Absolute holiness through the love of God:** Jn. 13:34-35; II Cor. 7:1; Heb. 12:14; I Peter 1:15-16.

9. **Resurrection of the dead:** I Cor. 15:52; I Thess. 4:16; II Cor. 5:10; Rev. 20:13.

10. **The translation of the saints:** Dan. 12:3; I Cor. 15:51; Phil. 3:21; I Jn. 3:2-3.

11. **The second coming of Jesus:** II Peter 3:10; Titus 2:13; Rev. 1:7, 22:16.

12. **The thousand years, the new heaven, and new earth:** Rev. 20:4-7; 21:1, II Peter 3:13.

13. **Jesus is God, God is Jesus:** Isa. 9:6, Luke 2:11, I Tim. 3:16; Jn. 1:13-14.

14. **Baptize in the name of Jesus Christ:** Acts 2:38; Gal. 3:27; Acts 4:10-12, 22:16.

15. **Water only for sacrament:** Mark 9:41; Dan 1:12; Luke 22:20; John 19:34-35.

16. **Water always has been used for the salvation with the blood:** Heb. 9:18-20; Num 19:13; I Jn 5:6-8; I Peter 3:20.

17. **Sin not against the Holy Ghost:** Matt. 12:31; Mark 3:28-29; Heb. 6:4-8, 10:26-31.

18. **Elect and election:** Isa. 45:4; Isa. 65:9; Matt. 24:22; Rom. 11:7.

19. **Foreknowledge:** Jer. 1:5; Prov. 22:3; Rom. 11:2; I Peter 1:2-20.

20. **Pre-existence of Jesus:** Isa. 9:6; Micah 5:2; Jn. 8:58; Jn. 17:24.

21. **Christ redeemer always:** Psa. 130:8; Hos. 13:14; Luke 1:68

22. **Signs:** Isa. 7:14; Ex. 4:8; Luke 2:12 ; Acts 2 :19.

23. **The Passover forever, a type of Christ:** Ex. 12:24; I Peter 1:19; I Cor. 5:7-8.

24. **Unity of God's people:** Psa. 133:1; Psa. 81:11; Rom. 12:16; I Cor. 12:20.

There are five Core Values that define a Hebrew Pentecostal believer. The values presented here are not all inclusive of the ultimate requirements for believers, but serve to synthesize the key elements; to establish a baseline of basic beliefs that are common among all Hebrew Pentecostal believers. These values are "core" because they are essential to salvation and Biblically substantiated. There are many other values that we and others subscribe to but are not defined in the same way. The five Core Values are as follows:

- **Observances**
- **Baptism**
- **Diet**
- **Indwelling of the Holy Spirit**
- **Oneness of the Creator / Trinity**

Observances

Our observances are core because they clearly separate us from much of the Christian world both in terms of the specific things that we observe and/or the reasons for those observances. The majority of the Christian Churches have followed the dictates of the Roman Catholic Church in accepting a regiment of celebrations that are non-biblical. Good examples are Christmas, Easter, St. Valentine's Day etc. Although these days are held up to be religious in concept, none of them can be found in the Holy Scriptures. Their origins are well known and documented in history, but there is no mandate from the Holy Scriptures to observe them.

On the other hand, the observances of our church are deeply rooted in the Word of God. We have concluded as Peter did in **Act 5:29** [1]*that it is better obey God rather than man.* Man's selected observances have no particular consequence for non-observance whereas God's commanded observances have very definite consequences for non-observance; a substantial difference in itself. Let us look at some of the observances established by God.

Baptism

An Important Step

Baptism is a Core Value because it is a sacred sacrament recognized for its particular importance and significance. It is often recognized as part of the first step toward salvation. Peter says in Acts 2:38 that the steps are "repentance" followed by "baptism". Water baptism is a ritual bath and has the effect of "remitting" sins. It is a form of renewal in that one is submerged into a watery grave and rises from that grave a new creature Romans 6:4. Further, since through the first man Adam death entered into all, unless we be born again of water and the Holy

---

[1] All Biblical references are from the King James Version

Ghost, we cannot enter into the kingdom of Heaven. That makes baptism an essential part and absolute necessity to salvation.

Indwelling of Holy Spirit

Although many Pentecostals believe in the indwelling of the Holy Spirit as a condition of salvation, there are many denominations who observe the 7th day Sabbath, eat clean etc., but do not believe in the indwelling of the Holy Spirit. Again, this is a defining characteristic and evidence of a spiritual conversion for Hebrew Pentecostal believers and therefore a Core Value. As in the Old Testament, the Ark was the repository for the presence of God and was evidenced by a pillar of cloud by day and a pillar of fire by night, so are true believers transformed as the repository of the Holy Spirit that physically dwells in us (1 Cor 6:19 *know ye not that your body is the temple of the Holy Ghost which is in you*) and is further identified by the power that is attendant with it. (Acts 1:8. . . and ye shall receive power after that the Holy Ghost is come upon you:). As Hebrew Pentecostals, we not only believe in the existence of the Holy Spirit but the personal physical inhabitance of that spirit once we are converted.

Oneness of Creator

Trinity Separates Christians

A significant difference between Hebrew Pentecostals and other Christian believers is our position on the Trinity. The entire Christian world is unified on the concept of "God in three persons", Father, Son, and Holy Ghost". They further believe that these three persons are separate, independent entities that cooperate in some fashion. Many who believe in the Trinity are surprised, perhaps shocked, to learn that the idea of divine beings existing as trinities or triads long predated Christianity, having its roots embedded in Greek culture. Fewer still understand how the Trinity doctrine came to be accepted - several centuries after the Bible was completed!

The Greek Influence

It is important to point out that many historians and religious scholars attest to the influence of Greek or Platonic philosophy in the development and acceptance of the Trinity doctrine in the fourth century. Nevertheless, some Bible translators of past centuries were so zealous to find support for their belief in the Trinity in Scripture that they literally added it. A case in point is 1 John 5:7-8 a scripture verse that does not appear in any Greek manuscript. It was added to the *Latin* manuscripts, probably first in North Africa, being mentioned by Cyprian of Carthage in 258 and Augustine about the year 400.[2] It is referred to in Biblical Studies as the Comma Johannine (*a short clause of a sentence relevant to the writing of John*) [3] and is the subject of much debate even today. The fourteenth principle of the Guiding Star details our position declaring that "Jesus is God and God is Jesus.

---

[2] Bruce M. Metzger, The Text of the New Testament: Its Transmission, Corruption, and Restoration, 2d ed. Oxford University 1968, p. 101

[3] **The** Comma Johanneum **as a Textual Problem;** by C.L. BOLT

Conclusion

The Core Values are tools to assist you in sharing our beliefs with others. It is important that we along with others understand that there are a variety of issues that enter into developing a proper relationship with God, but the Core Values serve to focus our attention on the most compelling issues guiding our worship and service, as well as those issues that differentiates us from others. They are essential to salvation and set's a baseline for other issues that will bring you even closer to God in your spiritual relationship with Him. In our mission to expand the body of Christ, it is often difficult if not impossible to determine if the organizations or people we are pursuing are in line with our beliefs. Using the Core Values as a yardstick will insure that at least initially, you will be in company with those who are much like yourself. Notwithstanding, this should not be our total focus as the body of Christ is open to all people regardless of their beliefs. It does however make your job a little easier in witnessing to them.

FEAST OF TRUMPETS

Introduction

This first day of the seventh month is a Sabbath. It is a memorial of blowing of trumpets; a holy convocation. A convocation is a called out public meeting or rehearsal (Strong's Dictionary). The trumpet was used in the Bible to call attention to specific situations. As we celebrate this Feast of the Lord, we look forward to its future prophetical fulfillment by the Lord Jesus Christ. Let us also take time to look at the present application of this feast.

Memory Verse *John 5:28 Marvel not* at this: for the hour is coming, in the which all that are in the graves shall hear his voice.

Biblical Application

I Corinthians 14 addresses the importance of sounds and words being able to be understood. There are many kinds of voices in the world and none of them is without significance. For example, the sound of the trumpet was used if Israel was going to war against the enemy. If the trumpet gave an uncertain sound, who shall prepare himself to battle. One day the Lord sounded his trumpet in our lives for a specific purpose. Many of us attempted to ignore the sound of the Lord's trumpet calling us to repentance. However, the voice of God was persistent. Others didn't immediately recognize the significance of the Spirit of God drawing them. They did not understand that it was the Lord working in them. None of us decided to come to Christ on our own. The Scripture declares: there is none that understandeth, there is none that seeketh after God. Many today continue to harden their hearts and stiffen their necks to the call of God. However; we must continue to cry aloud and spare not, lift our voices like a trumpet and show people their transgressions and sins. For the hour is coming in the which all that are in the graves shall hear his voice and shall come forth; they that have done good, unto the resurrection of life; and they that have done evil unto the resurrection of damnation.

- The voice of God came to your life. *Ezekiel 16:1-9; Isaiah 1:16-20.*
- The Father draws us. *Proverbs 16:1; Jeremiah 31: 3; John 6:44, 65.*
- Now we know his voice. John 10:1-5.
- All will hear his voice. *John 5:28-29; I Thessalonians 4:13-18, Leviticus 23:24.*

Everyday Life Application

Where were you when the Lord began to draw you? Are you willing to extend grace and mercy to others such as was extended to you?

THY GOD; MY GOD

Introduction

Elimelech and Naomi took their two sons from Bethlehem-judah to live in the country of Moab due to a famine in the land. According to *Judges 11:24* and *Numbers 21:29*, the Moabites worshipped the false god Chemosh. Naomi's husband Elimelech died in Moab, as did her two sons; after they married Moabite women. The Moabite daughters in law of Naomi were Ruth and Orpah. When the famine ended in Bethlehem-judah, Naomi decided to return home. Ruth insisted on returning with her mother in law despite efforts by Naomi to get her to stay in Moab.

Memory Verse *Ruth 1:16* And Ruth said, Intreat me not to leave thee, or to return from following after thee: for whither thou goest, I will go; and where thou lodgest, I will lodge: thy people shall be my people, and thy God my God:

Biblical Application

Ruth made life changing decisions primarily based on her faith in the Almighty God. Boaz was a wealthy family member of Elimelech and a follower of the Almighty. He recognized Ruth's faith and trust in God in leaving her mother, father, and the land of her nativity. The Lord used Boaz to bless the faithfulness of Ruth. Boaz spoke blessings over her life and blessed her as she gleaned. He told the young men who were harvesting to allow handfuls of purpose (bundles of grain) to fall in the field so she would have more than just the loose pieces of barley. The Lord often recognizes the faithfulness of believers by using others to bless us. Boaz recognized that Ruth was blessed of the Lord as a virtuous woman. Ruth also demonstrated her faith in God through remaining faithful to Naomi. She eventually gave birth to Obed the father of Jesse who was the father of David and entered the lineage of Jesus Christ.

- Ruth forsook family to follow God. *Ruth 2:8-16; Matthew 10:29, 34-40, 12:46-50; Mark 10:28-31.*
- Ruth was known to be a virtuous woman. *Ruth 3:8-12; Proverbs 12:4, 31:10-31.*
- Let us be faithful servants. *Ruth 4: 14-15; Matthew 25:14-30.*
- Ruth was in the lineage of the Jesus Christ. *Ruth 4:17-22; Matthew 1:1-6.*

Everyday Life Application

How has the Lord rewarded your faithfulness to him and his people?

What motivates you to remain faithful when others fall away or things get tough?

THE DAY OF ATONEMENT

Introduction

This 10th day of the seventh month is a Sabbath of rest in which the we are commanded to afflict our souls by a statute forever (Lev 16:31). A restriction of no work was also given for this day. The Bible declared it a day in which the priest made an atonement for you, to cleanse you, that ye may be clean from all your sins before the LORD. On this day the high priest entered the veil into the holy place before the mercy seat to make an atonement with a sin offering for himself, his household (blood of a bullock), and all the congregation of Israel (blood of a kid goat). Two rams were also used for a burnt offering for the priest and the congregation. A scapegoat was required in which the high priest confessed over him all the iniquities of the children of Israel, and all their transgressions in all their sins, putting them upon the head of the goat, and then sent him away by the hand of a fit man into the wilderness. The goat would bear upon him all their iniquities unto a land not inhabited.

Memory Verse *Hebrews 2:9* But we see Jesus, who was made a little lower than the angels for the suffering of death, crowned with glory and honour; that he by the grace of God should taste death for every man.

Biblical Application

The high priest alone was permitted to enter the veil into the holy place to make the atonement. Jesus Christ was made a little lower than the angels, forasmuch as the children are partakers of flesh and blood, he himself likewise took part of the same, that through death he might destroy him that had the power of death. That is the devil and to deliver them who through fear of death were all their lifetime subject to bondage. By the grace of God Jesus suffered and tasted death to make the atonement for us. The Lord laid on him the sins and iniquities of us all. As Jesus hung on the cross from the sixth hour until the ninth hour there was darkness over all the earth, the sun was darkened and the veil of the temple was rent in the midst before he gave up the ghost. Jesus Christ is our merciful, faithful high priest that made the atonement for us once and for all. He ever lives to make intercession for us. Having therefore, brethren, boldness to enter into the holiest by the blood of Jesus. By a new and living way, which he hath consecrated for us, through the veil, that is to say, his flesh. Let us draw near with a true heart in full assurance of faith, having our hearts sprinkled from an evil conscience, and our bodies washed with pure water. Let us hold fast the profession of our faith without wavering; for he is faithful that promised.

- The Day of Atonement. *Leviticus 16:1-34.*
- Jesus was made a little lower than angels. *Hebrews 2:1-18.*
- The veil was rent in twain. *Matthew 27: 26-54; Hebrews 10: 1-27.*

Everyday Life Application

What things are you committed to daily to hold fast the profession of your faith without wavering? How does not forsaking the assembly of ourselves together in corporate worship help you hold fast?

FEAST OF TABERNACLES

Introduction

The Bible also refers to this feast as the Feast of Ingathering. This feast occurred at the end of the year when labors (product or property) were gathered out of the field (Strong's Dictionary). Most of us no longer practice an agrarian lifestyle. Our harvest is commonly a result of labor in our current area of employment. Regardless of your profession and source of income, it is the Lord who provides that which we are blessed to gather in.

Memory Verse *Exodus 23:16* And the feast of harvest, the firstfruits of thy labours, which thou hast sown in the field: and the feast of ingathering, which is in the end of the year, when thou hast gathered in thy labours out of the field.

Biblical Application

In Deuteronomy 8, the Lord told Israel to remember all the way which he had led them forty years in the wilderness. He allowed them to suffer hunger, fed them with manna, and chastened them; but their raiment waxed not old and their foot did not swell. The Lord warned them about when he was going to bring them into the good land. He told them they would eat bread without scarceness and not lack anything in it. God commanded them to bless him when they had eaten and were full; for the good land which he had given them. He said to beware lest they should forget the Lord in not keeping his commandments, and his judgments, and his statutes. The Lord also told them not to say in their heart that my power and the might of my hand hath gotten me this wealth. In our modern, economically prosperous society; we are more educated than ever. According to the U.S. Census Bureau in 2016, 89% of Americans age 25 and older have graduated high school or equivalent and 33% have at least a bachelor's degree. [4]We have many conveniences that keep us comfortable night and day. Some of us have jobs and income we never thought possible. As we rejoice and enjoy the blessings that the Lord has provided; let us keep them in the perspective of the Scriptures. Let us remember the Lord our God; it is he that hath given thee power to get wealth. It is the Lord who gives us knowledge and wisdom to prosper in our field. The Lord is the one who opens doors and makes ways for us. During this Feast of Ingathering we rejoice in all that the Lord has enabled us to harvest.

- Remember the provision is from the Lord. *Deuteronomy 8:1-20; Proverbs 10:22.*
- The Feast of Tabernacles. *Exodus 23:14-17; Deuteronomy 16:13-17.*
- God gives us ability and prosperity in our labours. *Exodus 31:1-6, 35:30-35; I Kings 7:13-14; II Chronicles 2:13-14; Isaiah 28:23-29; Daniel 1:4, 9, 17-20.*

Everyday Life Application

How has the Lord blessed you in the labours you have gathered in? What have you done to show your gratitude to the Lord for his provision?

---

[4] United States Census Bureau https://www.census.gov/newsroom/press-releases/2017/cb17-51.html

FEAST OF TABERNACLES LAST GREAT DAY

Introduction

This last great day of this feast points prophetically to the new heavens and new earth when the tabernacle of God will be with men and he will dwell with them. They shall be his people and God himself shall be with them, and be their God. We celebrate this feast and look forward to that day with great anticipation.

Memory Verse *Leviticus 23:36* Seven days ye shall offer and offering made by fire unto the Lord: on the eighth day shall be a holy convocation unto you: and ye shall offer and offering made by fire unto the Lord: it is a solemn assembly; and ye shall do no servile work therein.

Biblical Application

In the last day, that great day of the feast, Jesus stood and cried, saying, if any man thirst, let him come unto me and drink. He that believeth on me as the Scripture hath said, out of his belly shall flow rivers of living water. This spake he of the Spirit, which those that believe on him receives. Through receiving the Holy Ghost, we become the temple of God and God lives in us. What a privilege to have the very presence of God in us to teach us and guide us into all truth. While we enjoy the benefits of the Spirit of truth in us here on earth, we realize that it will be much more glorious in the future. We look with excited anticipation for the day in the new heavens and new earth when the tabernacle of God will be with men. Beloved, now are we the sons of God, and it doth not yet appear what we shall be: but we know that, when he shall appear, we shall be like him; for we shall see him as he is. And every man that hath this hope in him purifieth himself, even as he is pure. For now, we see through a glass, darkly; but then face to face: now I know in part; but then shall I know even as also I am known. Let us be steadfast, unmovable, always abounding in the work of the Lord, for as much as you know that your labour is not in vain in the Lord.

- The body of Christ is the current temple of God. *John 7:37-40*
- *I Corinthians 3:16-17, 6:19-20, 12:12-27; II Corinthians 4:6-7.*
- The future tabernacle of God. *Revelation 21:1-27, 22:1-5.*
- Let us hold fast unto the end. *Matthew 24:4-13; Hebrews 3:6, 12-14.*
- We rejoice and keep the Feast. *Leviticus 23:33-44.*

Everyday Life Application

How did your life change when you became the temple of God? What steps are you taking daily to ensure that you endure unto the end?

THE ART OF PERSUASION

Introduction

Satan who has come down to earth having great wrath, set in motion a master strategy to separate us from God. His art of persuasion enabled him in drawing a host of angels to make war in heaven. Satan's ability to persuade is being used to condition humanity to accept unrighteousness as a normal part of life. The Church must be aware of the Devil's ability of persuasion, so that members will avoid becoming entangled in a sinful lifestyle. Satan is a master at inducing small amounts of negative stimuli, giving the recipient time to adjust and acclimate that behavior into their daily routine. This involves giving just enough to not seem harmful, and therefore desensitizing the recipient to the true intent of what is being introduced. Desensitizing as Webster defines it, is "to make one emotionally insensitive or callous *specifically*: to extinguish an emotional response (as of fear, anxiety, or guilt) to stimuli that formerly induced it i.e. the fear of the Lord".

Memory Verse: *II Corinthians 11:3* But I fear, lest by any means, as the serpent beguiled Eve through his subtilty, so your minds should be corrupted from the simplicity that is in Christ.

Biblical Application

In the first book of the Bible, the Scripture describes Satan as the serpent that's subtler than any beast of the field which the Lord had made. As Satan engages Eve in a conversation, the tone does not suggest an aggressive attack but more of a question. "Yea, hath God said, Ye shall not eat of every tree of the garden?" (*Genesis 3:1) These* simple words spoken, coupled with Eve's observation that the tree was good for food, allowed the serpent to be successful in convincing

Eve and Adam to accept a fruit that was forbidden by God. Paul describes him this way, . . . "for Satan himself is transformed into an angel of light" (2 Corinthians 11:14). Satan is still at work conditioning society to accept unrighteousness as the norm. You can see this play out in daily TV shows as we see more and more same sex couples and provocative story lines being promoted. Our children are also bombarded with cartoons that promote disrespect towards parents, and cartoons that promote violence, even towards authority figures; all this to bring us to a place where we will call evil good and good evil.

Beware of Seducing Spirits	Earnestly Contending for the Faith
Numbers 25:1-3 *Proverbs 7:6-23*	*Numbers 25: 4-18* *Proverbs7: 24-27*
Acts 20:28-30	*Acts 20:31-32*
I Timothy 4:1-5	*I Timothy 4:6-11*
Jude 1: 4 *Isa 14:12-7* *Rev 12:7-12*	*Jude 1:21-25*

Everyday Life Application

What other mechanisms has Satan used in conditioning this world to accept unrighteousness?

How do we become aware of the things that we have become [5]desensitized to?

What can we, as the elect of God, do to offset his agenda?

Author: *Evangelist Patricia Powell*

---

[5] https://www.merriam-webster.com/dictionary/desensitize

POTENTIAL

Introduction

The book of Daniel begins with prophecy fulfilled. Jerusalem has been destroyed, the invading Babylonian army has taken the city and the people. Babylon, being one of those historical nations of the Bible, but also respected in modern education, has arrived and conquered Israel as God said they would. The text goes on to say that much was stolen from God's house. There were various, intricate, precious vessels that Babylon stole, the incredible silver, bronze and gold, fine cedar, all the resources that David collected and passed to Solomon that were dedicated to the church for worship. Along with these precious vessels, Babylon also stole another commodity; the people.

Memory Verse *Daniel 1:3* "And the king spake unto Ashpenaz the master of his eunuchs, that he should bring certain of the children of Israel, and of the king's seed and of the princes"

Biblical Application

Nebuchadnezzar took possession of *certain* of the children of Israel. Namely, Shadarach, Meshach, and Abednego as well as Daniel. These individuals were earmarked for greatness. We later found out they were endued spiritually, and morally; they had incredible potential.

- Unlocked potential. *Daniel 1:4.*
- The king expected greatness of them. *Daniel 1:5.*
- Leaders should develop and encourage growth especially among youth. *II Timothy 1:6.*
- Providing the push for greatness. *II Timothy 3:14-17.*

Everyday Life Application

Good seeds grow with nurturance. Find ways to nurture youth and natural strengths in all you encounter.

Author: *Elder David T. Brand Jr. MA LPC*

Source: https://www.psychologytoday.com/us/blog/in-control/201911/youll-never-reach-your-potential

LET US CLEANSE OURSELVES

Introduction

In today's society, the number of men and women who agree with premarital cohabitation, non-marital childbearing, same-sex relations, and adult premarital sex is increasing [6](CDC, 2016). Television programs, movies, and the internet abound with all manner of immorality and sin. As iniquity abounds, it is important for the people of God not to become desensitized to sin. As followers of Christ we must hold fast to the Word of God and reject all manner of ungodliness.

Memory Verse *II Corinthians 7:1* Having therefore these promises, dearly beloved, let us cleanse ourselves from all filthiness of the flesh and spirit, perfecting holiness in the fear of God.

Biblical Application

Our sanctification is a result of the Holy Ghost coming into our lives and us making deliberate decisions to obey God's Word. Based on the exhortation to cleanse ourselves from all filthiness of the flesh, we must be proactive in our choices. This includes abstaining from ungodly things on the internet and television and not partaking in filthy conversations at work or school. The Bible warns against being yoked together with unbelievers. Our close relationships should not be with unrighteous people. We are blessed if we walk not in the counsel of the ungodly, don't stand in the way of sinners, or sit in the seat of the scornful. In order to perfect holiness we must renew our

---

[6] CDC. National Health Statistics Reports Number 19 March, 17, 2016. Trends in Attitudes About Marriage, Childbearing, and Sexual Behavior: United States, 2002, 2006–2010, and 2011–2013. Daughtery, J. & Copen, C.

minds with the Word of God day by day. God's Word is truth and has the power to sanctify us.

- Come out from among them. *II Corinthians 6:14-18, 7:1.*
- Purify yourself and be a child of God. *I John 3:2-10.*
- Possess your vessel in sanctification and honour. *I Thessalonians 4:1-7*
- Abstain from fleshly lusts. *I Peter 2:11-17.*
- Mortify your earthly members. *Colossians 3:5-17.*

Everyday Life Application

What are some things you can do to avoid entering into sexual temptation?

How has the world attempted to silence the church about speaking out against sin?

DILIGENCE

Introduction

Diligence is defined in Your Dictionary as "determination and careful effort". We all strive to be our best. Being diligent is an essential skill in all aspects of life. Diligence is the opposite of slothfulness. A diligent person is described as attentive, industrious, conscientious, thorough; not idle, not negligent or slothful. We have a desire to be successful in all our endeavors, but instead of being diligent some would rather take the easy way out to accomplish their goals. The Book of Proverbs records many warnings against slothfulness, and throughout Scripture we find instructions to live with diligence. Diligence is a quality that God instills in believers in order to experience true fulfillment.

Memory Verse *Proverbs 20:11* Even a child is known by his doings, whether his work be pure, and whether it be right.

Biblical Application

Throughout Scripture, we are challenged to work diligently and to do all things in a manner that brings glory to God. According to Scripture, God takes the topic of diligence seriously. Diligence is highly esteemed and valued by God. Apparently, God knows the many vices of the heart, and He warns us to guard our hearts with diligence against them. Diligence, or persistence, is the virtue which acts contrary to slothfulness. The Israelites were instructed by God to diligently "Remember God Every Day" in the land whither they were going - the Promised Land which flowed with milk and honey. *Deuteronomy 4:9, 6: 6-7,17, 28:1.*

- All Scripture must be diligently studied and accurately applied. *II Timothy 2:15.*
- Be doers of the word, and not hearers only. *James 1:22.*
- The diligent will be rewarded with countless blessings: *Proverbs 4:23, 10:4, 11:27, 12:24, 27, 13:4, 21:5; 22:29, 23:1-3, 27:23.*
- The Apostle Peter encourages the brethren to be diligent in their faith and calling. *II Peter 1:5-7-9, 11.*

Everyday Life Application

Discuss some steps to be taken toward becoming diligent.

Author: *Evangelist Irene Crawford*

BLESSED ARE THE MERCIFUL

Introduction

Mercy in *Matthew 5:7* means to have compassion by word or deed, specifically by divine grace (Strong's Dictionary). Do you remember when you first realized that God's mercy was upon you? Many of us were ignorant of the righteous judgment we deserved as a result of our sins. According to the law, there were numerous sins that were punishable by death. If a child cursed or smote his father or mother, he was to be surely put to death. Men and women that committed adultery or witchcraft were also to be put to death. The punishment of death by stoning sometimes involved all of the congregation stoning the person. The law stated life for life, eye for eye, tooth for tooth, hand for hand, foot for foot, burning for burning, wound for wound, and stripe for stripe.

Memory Verse *Matthew 5:7* Blessed are the merciful: for they shall obtain mercy.

Biblical Application

Each one of us have sinned against the Lord and the wages our sin earned was death. However, the Lord had mercy on us through the punishment and sacrifice of Jesus Christ for our sins. Sacrifices and offering for sin were common in the old covenant. These sacrifices were temporary and could not take away sin. The weightier matters of the law were judgment, mercy, and faith. When the Pharisees asked the disciples of Jesus why he ate with publicans and sinners, he revealed who he came to call. He said he would have mercy and not sacrifice and that he came to call sinners to repentance. As we reflect on the mercy that God extended to us, let us be careful to extend mercy to others.

- Judgment by the law. *Exodus 21: 1,12-25 22: 18; Leviticus 20:8-11, 21, 24:10-23.*
- The Lord is merciful. *Lamentations 3: 21-26; Luke 1:47-50, Matthew 9:10-13, 12:1-13; Titus 3:3-6 James 5:11, Ephesians 2:1-5.*
- Show mercy to others. *Micah 6:6-8; Luke 10:30-37; Romans 12:8, James 2:13, 3:17.*

Everyday Life Application.

How have you extended mercy to others? What else can you do to show someone the mercy of God?

THE KINGDOM'S PREEMINENCE

Introduction

From the onset of His ministry, it is undeniable that Jesus put a premium on the Kingdom of God, fervently urging its preeminence in the lives of mankind. Jesus made statements that offended many individuals, and even today some are offended. But it was foretold He would be a rock of offense, a stone of stumbling, and many would fall, and be broken. This lesson shows the Kingdom of God must be paramount above all that men hold dear in this present evil world.

Memory Verse *Matthew 11:6* Blessed is he whosoever shall not be offended in me.

Biblical Application

How important is gaining entrance into The Kingdom? Jesus says, "If your hand or your foot offends you, cut it off. If your eye offends you, pluck it out; for it is better one enters the Kingdom crippled or blind than be cast into the lake of fire." Sounds extreme! But, the context of such an illustration wasn't that absurd in ancient times. Its aim is to insight a sense of urgency. Such a statement is not to be taken in the literal sense of course. The technical term for such an expression is called hyperbole: an "Over the Top" statement to exaggerate a point. It's like a parent who says to a child, "If you do that again, I'm going to skin you alive." The child knows their parent is speaking figuratively, nonetheless, they get the seriousness of the matter. Jesus tells a rich young man, "Go sell all and come and follow me." Is Jesus asking too much? One man asked to bury a family member before following Him, Jesus replies, "Let the dead bury the dead." Is this going too far? Jesus stressed the importance of gaining entrance in the Kingdom at all cost, even over our most valued possessions, such as family, social status, earthly possessions, and yes, even more valuable than the loss of a hand or foot. We must be wholly sold out for the hope of gaining eternal life.

- Christ, a rock of offense. *Isaiah 8:14-15; Matthew 23:25-33; Luke 4:17-28, 1 Peter 2:6-8.*
- We must forsake all. *Luke 14:25-33; Luke 18:28-30; Hebrews 11:24-27.*

Everyday Life Application

What is the ultimate cost of following Christ?

Author: *Minister Robert O. Johnson*

BURN WITHIN US

Introduction

The Bible declares, "Verily thou art a God that hidest thyself, O God of Israel, the Saviour". In his prophecy about the coming Messiah, Isaiah asks, "Who hath believed our report? and to whom is the arm of the LORD revealed"? *(Isa 53:1).* Another prophecy referenced by Jesus and Paul in the New Testament states: *(Isa 6:9-10)* "Go, and tell this people, Hear ye indeed, but understand not; and see ye indeed, but perceive not. Make the heart of this people fat, and make their ears heavy, and shut their eyes; lest they see with their eyes, and hear with their ears, and understand with their heart, and convert, and be healed".

Many people hear the Word of God, but shut their eyes and heart in unbelief. In a time when some churches have replaced the preaching of the Word of God with concerts and theatrics, let us remember the words of Christ, *(Mat 13:16-17)* ". . .blessed are your eyes, for they see: and your ears, for they hear. For verily I say unto you, That many prophets and righteous men have desired to see those things which ye see, and have not seen them; and to hear those things which ye hear, and have not heard them"

Memory Verse *Luke 24:32* And they said one to another, Did not our heart burn within us, while he talked with us by the way, and while he opened to us the Scriptures?

Biblical Application

Mary Magdalene, Joanna, Mary the mother of James, and other women brought spices to the sepulcher of Jesus. They were perplexed when Jesus was gone. They did not remember what Jesus previously told them about Jonah and his resurrection. Two men in shining garments (angels) at the sepulcher explained that Jesus was risen. When they returned to the apostles with the news; even they did not believe it. Peter even went to the sepulcher himself and found that Jesus was gone and wondered what happened. On the road to Emmaus Jesus appeared to Cleopas and another unnamed disciple. However; it was not revealed to them who he was. Despite teaching them for over three years, the disciples had their own ideas about the Messiah redeeming Israel. Jesus expounded to them from Moses and all the prophets the things concerning himself. Their heart burned within them as he opened them the Scriptures. As the Holy Ghost gives us the revelation of who Jesus is and reveals to us the Scriptures, we must be careful to walk therein.

- Abide not in unbelief. *Luke 24: 1-45; Hebrews 4:1-2.*

- The Lord opens our hearts. *Acts 16:11-15, 8:26-39, 28:16-31; John 12:34-43; Matthew 13:10-17.*

- Walk in the light of the Word. *Jeremiah 6:16-19; Isaiah 8:19-20; Psalm 119: 97-106.*

Everyday Life Application

Have you experienced understanding and spiritual growth as you adjust your lifestyle according to the Word of God?

Does your heart burn within you as the Word is preached or taught?

CALL UPON THE LORD

Introduction

In this life, as believer's we are encouraged to provide for ourselves, to be good stewards over our resources, to take care of our bodies with exercise and good eating habits. We are also encouraged to live disciplined lives, to be good moral agents, to live peaceably with all men. In summary, we are to pay attention to the details of every aspect of our lives. But, no matter how well we prepare, how well we manage, and how disciplined we are, there will always be things and circumstances that happen to us beyond our control. Whether it be a car wreck, a virus, a natural disaster, etc., we will need assistance beyond our ability to supply for ourselves.

Memory Verse *Psalm 124:8* Our help is in the name of the LORD, who made heaven and earth.

Biblical Application

My brothers and sisters, we have the resource of calling upon the Lord for his intercession and intervention in our affairs. For *Psalm 34:15* says, "The eyes of the Lord are upon the righteous, and his ears are open unto their cry." There are times things happen without warning and beyond our control, but there are times we have been guilty of being the reason unfavorable things have come upon us. But even in those times, God does not abandon us. We have this assurance he can right our wrongs. We have the assurance that he hears us.

- The power of his name. *Proverbs 18:10; Philippians 2: 9-11.*
- The Psalmists' cry. *Psalms 18:3-6; Psalms 116:1-4; Psalms 34: 6-17.*

- Faith is cricital. *Matthew 14: 28-31; Luke 18: 35-43; Mark 9:17-23.*

Everyday Life Application

Give specific testimonies of when you called on the name of Lord and he responded.

Author: *Elder James Taylor, Jr.*

A MIND TO WORK

Introduction

Nehemiah was a cupbearer to King Artaxerxes of Persia in the post Babylonian exile period. As [7]cupbearer, he was responsible to deliver the king's drink to him and ensure that it was free from poison [8](ISBE). This was a highly trusted position and allowed daily interaction with the king. The Lord, who knows the end from the beginning, had sovereignly placed Nehemiah in that position. Nehemiah maintained solid moral and emotional character and the Lord gave him favor in the king's sight. Nehemiah served the king of Persia faithfully as his profession. However, the true motivation of Nehemiah was his reverence for the Lord and His Word.

Memory Verse *Nehemiah 4:6* So built we the wall; and all the wall was joined together unto the half thereof: for the people had a mind to work.

Biblical Application

The love Nehemiah had for God caused him to take action. After hearing about the distress of Jerusalem, he prayed, fasted, and went to work. He prayed a sincere prayer of confession, repentance, asking for the mercy of God based on his Word and for favor in the king's sight. After being equipped by God through the king, Nehemiah used wisdom and faith to accomplish the task of rebuilding the wall. His words and action inspired others to have a mind to work for the Lord.

---

[7]

https://www.biblestudytools.com/encyclopedias/isbe/cupbearer.html

[8] International Standard Bible Encyclopedia. (ISBE).

After rebuilding the wall in 52 days, he didn't stop there. Nehemiah instituted many reforms facilitating a return to keeping the Word of God. Some of the demonstrations of Nehemiah's faith included overcoming ridicule and discouragement, ending usury toward brethren, demonstrating personal generosity, restoration of Feast observance, tithes, Sabbath observance, forbidding intermarriage with pagans, and reverence for the sanctuary.

- Nehemiah's prayer. *Nehemiah 1:4-11.*
- God's favor. *Nehemiah 2:4-9.*
- Faith in action. *James 2:14-22; Nehemiah 2:18-20, 4:7-20, 5:1-12.*
- Restoration of proper worship. *Nehemiah 8:9-12, 10:32-37, 13:1-31.*

Everyday Life Application

How are you working to establish and maintain the kingdom of God through your local church? What can you improve in your professional life to facilitate gaining the favor of God with them?

SERVE HIM IN SINCERITY AND IN TRUTH

Introduction

Joshua was 110 years old when he died. Before his death he gathered all the tribes of Israel to Shechem, including the elders, heads, judges, and officers. In his final exhortation, he reminded them of how the Lord had delivered them for generations. Joshua told them to choose whom they would serve and warned them of the consequences if they forsook the Lord. He made it clear that he and his house chose to serve the Lord.

Memory Verse *Joshua 24:14* Now therefore fear the LORD, and serve him in sincerity and in truth: and put away the gods which your fathers served on the other side of the flood, and in Egypt; and serve ye the LORD.

Biblical Application

We have a choice to make. Ungodliness abounds around us; people call good evil and evil good. Either we will compromise with the world and forsake God or we will fear the Lord and serve him in sincerity and truth. To fear(revere) and serve(work) the Lord in sincerity(integrity) and truth(stability) involves living a lifestyle of Biblical integrity regardless of where you are and who you are with (Strong's Dictionary). We must choose to make personal decisions daily to obey the Word of God and resist ungodly influences. It includes being sober and vigilant; resisting the adversary steadfast in the faith. Let us put on the whole armor of God daily, so that we may be able to stand against the wiles (method/trickery) of the devil (Strong's Dictionary). This includes using the shield of faith which we use to quench all the fiery darts of the wicked. Our offensive weapon is the sword of the Spirit; the Word of God.

- Make a choice to serve the Lord. *Joshua 24:1-31.*

- Avoid the snares, traps, scourges, and thorns. *Joshua 23:1-16; Ephesians 6:10-18.*
- Serve the Lord in sincerity and truth. *Psalm 51:6; Titus 2:9-13; II Corinthians 4:1-2; Revelation 3:15-19.*

Everyday Life Application

Be open and honest with the Lord about your daily struggles, repent, and pray for deliverance.

BLESSED ARE THEY THAT MOURN

Introduction

Mourn in *Matthew 5:4* means to grieve (Strong's Dictionary). There are many situations in this life that cause us to grieve. The death of a family member or friend is perhaps the most common. Words cannot describe the loss that we feel when someone close to us departs this life. Jesus experienced grief when Lazarus passed. When he saw Mary and the Jews weeping, he groaned in the spirit, was troubled, and wept. Mary Magdalene and the other disciples mourned and wept after the death of Jesus. While we mourn and experience grief at times in this life; it is important to realize that our hope is not in this life only, but in the resurrection.

Memory Verse *Matthew 5:4* Blessed are they that mourn: for they shall be comforted.

Biblical Application

Because the Christian's hope is not only in this world, then we must also mourn at the realization of sine within us. The Bible gives examples of mourning at the realization and acknowledgement of our sins. True repentance for instance includes confessing and turning away from our sins. He that covereth his sins shall not prosper: but whoso confesseth and forsaketh them shall have mercy. In order to draw nigh to God, sinners are to cleanse their hands, purify their hearts, be afflicted, mourn and weep as they humble themselves to the Lord. This affliction and mourning are a result of the conviction the Holy Ghost brings to our hearts. We realize that we have sinned against God who is righteous and holy, but still loves us. Peter wept bitterly when he remembered the words of Jesus and realized that he had denied Christ. The Holy Ghost brings Godly sorrow and repentance unlike the adversary which attempts to condemn us.

- Jesus and the disciples mourned. *John 11:21-38 , 20: 1-16.*
- God gives grace to the humble. *James 4:1-10; Proverbs 28:13.*
- Repent and make straight paths for your feet. *Hebrews 12:1-17; Matthew 3:1-12.*
- The Holy Ghost is our Comforter. *John 16:7-14; Isaiah 61:1-3.*

Everyday Life Application

If you are mourning after death or experiencing grief do not isolate yourself. Reach out to family, friends, or a counselor for help.

FAITH TRIED AND TESTED

Introduction

According to Strong's Concordance, the Greek word for Faith is *Pistis*. *Peíthō* is the root word for *Pístis* and involves obedience, but it is properly the result of God's persuasion. Faith is defined as the ability "to persuade or be persuaded" of what is trustworthy. Faith is a gift from God, and something that is exercised by people. In short, *Pistis* (faith) for the believer is "God's divine persuasion" – and therefore distinct from human belief (confidence), but yet involves it. The Lord continuously births faith in the yielded believer so they can know what He prefers, i.e. the persuasion of His will (*I John 5:4*). The Lord persuades the yielded believer to be confident in His preferred-will (*Galatians 5:10; II Timothy 1:12*). Tried is defined or used in various phrases to describe something that has proven effective or reliable. Test is defined as a procedure intended to establish the quality, performance, or reliability of something, especially before it is taken into widespread use.

Memory Verse: *Job 23:10* But he knoweth the way that I take: when he hath tried me, I shall come forth as gold.

Biblical Application

It's not a question of *whether* you'll face trials. It's just a matter of *when*. Take heart. No matter what you're facing today, or what you may have to face tomorrow, if you belong to God you can be confident there's a powerful purpose in your pain. An illness, unemployment, a fractured relationship—even the death of a loved one—happens for specific reasons; all wrapped up in God's sovereign, loving, nurturing embrace. The Book of Job clearly describes him as a man of great character. Job's holiness, Godly love for his children, uprightness and righteousness exemplified his perfection. Job's Piety and Godly fear were evident, yet, they did not prevent Satan from falsely accusing him. Job in all his afflictions refused to curse God, but chose to bless him.   The Apostle James tells us that in spite of the fact that trials can be severe and painful, we can see through our tears and realize by faith that God has a good intention in taking us through this sorrow. We can realize that the trial will produce perseverance and help to make us mature and complete. He exhorts us to be patience in affliction. (*James 1:3*)

Listed below are some Divine Methods used for testing believers:

- By demanding great sacrifices. *Genesis 22:1-2; Exodus 20:20.*
- By leading men in a difficult Way. *Deuteronomy 8:2, 13:3.*
- By giving opportunities for choice. *I Kings 3:5* In Gibeon the LORD appeared to Solomon in a dream by night and God said, "ask what I shall give thee".
  II Chronicles 32:31; Psalm 7:9; 11:5; 17:3.
- By proposing hard tasks. *John 6:5-6, 11:6.*
- By permitting men to suffer when in the pathway of duty. *Acts 16:23-24.*
- By permitting temptation. *James 1:1-3.*

Everyday Life Application

Believe God. Believe His promises. Trust and know that God knows what's best for you. He is able to keep and help you pass all of life's tests.

Author: *Evangelist Irene Crawford*

GOD IS A REAL GOOD FATHER

Introduction

Chris Tomlin an American contemporary Christian music artist, worship leader, and songwriter wrote these words:" I've heard a thousand stories of what they think you're like. But I've heard the tender whispers of love in the dead of night. And you tell me that you're pleased and that I'm never alone. You're a good- good father It's who you are, it's who you are, it's who you are. And I'm loved by you. It's who I am, it's who I am, it's who I am". Unfortunately, we have an enemy whose sole purpose is to separate us from God and what better way than to distort the way we see him. Today we will focus on the reality that we truly have a Good-Good Father!

Memory Verse *Jeremiah 31:3* The LORD hath appeared of old unto me, saying, Yea, I have loved thee with an everlasting love: therefore with lovingkindness have I drawn thee.

Biblical Application

From the very foundation of the world God had us in mind. When you look at the account of creation our comfort was always a priority. He put us in a garden with all the provisions needed to sustain ourselves. He placed us in an atmosphere conducive to the flesh being sustain, i.e. not freezing from cold air or burning from the sun rays. He has always shown a mindset of a good father. Un-fortunately Satan will always be close by waiting to turn disappointments and tragedies into indictments against God. He wants to portray him as a Father who does not care. However, when you take the time to read about God in his word and allow him to be Lord in your life you will find and experience the true heart of God for his people. We can look to the account of the woman caught in adultery and see the merciful hand of God. He did not condemn her, but told her to go and sin no more. That my friend is a Good-Good Father!

- Benefits of God being our Father. *Psalms 103: 1-14.*
- He is a Father that gives good gifts to his children *Luke 11: 11-13; Matthew 7: 7-11.*
- A good father will correct his children for their profit. *Hebrews 12: 1-13.*
- Our Father is preparing a special place for us. *John 14: 1-3; Revelation 21: 1-4.*

Everyday Life Application

Share with the class your experience where Satan challenged your belief that God is a Good Father.

How did you dispel that belief?

Author: *Evangelist Patricia Powell*

WHY STUDY?

Introduction

So, why study the Word of God? Isn't coming to Church and paying tithes enough? Isn't being on an auxiliary board or singing in the choir enough? While these things are good and profitable to the Church, they don't solely cultivate a personal intimacy and knowledge of God. Therefore, it's not enough; here's why? The bible reveals one repeated message about God, it is that He wants to be known. But how can anyone truly know someone without knowledge of them? Though we profess to be followers of Christ, how can anyone be a true disciple while unacquainted with the ways of their Master? The word study means devotion of time and attention to acquiring knowledge, by detailed investigation. The "Word" in Hebrew is "Dwar" meaning, "Doors to the House of knowledge." Jesus is the "Door"! This lesson stresses the importance of studying God's Word, so we can truly know Him intimately, and be followers of God as dear children.

Memory Verse *John 17:3* And this is life eternal, that they might know thee the only true God, and Jesus Christ, whom thou hast sent

Biblical Application

Why do we study God's word? One that we may be able to approve of what is that good, and acceptable, and perfect will of God. It is through this knowledge we can walk worthy of God who has called us to His Kingdom and glory. We also study to learn God's ways to obtain His promises and blessings. We study to rightly judge between clean and unclean, between holy and unholy. We study so we can walk as Jesus walked, as the truth is in Him, and bring forth fruit worthy of repentance. We also study to expose the apostasy of false worship and the lies of false preachers. As we can see there are numerous reasons as to why we must study the Word of God, albeit these are only a few.

Why study?

1. To know His Ways. *Exodus 33:12-23, Exodus 34:5-8.*
2. To walk worthy of God. *I Thessalonians 2:12, 4:1-5.*
3. To expose the enemy. *II Corinthians 11:3-4; 13-15.*
4. To walk not as the unbelievers. *Ephesians 4:17-24, Psalm 1.*
5. To worship in Spirit and Truth. *John 4:24.*
6. To give an answer. *Proverbs 15:28; Colossians 4:5-6.*
7. To be approved. *Matthew 7:21-27; I John 2:28, Tim 2:15.*

Everyday Life Application

Discuss how studying God's Word has helped change your life?

Author: *Minister Robert O. Johnson*

HE WILL NOT FAIL THEE NOR FORSAKE THEE

Introduction

When Moses was 120 years old and unable to come out or go in, he gave an exhortation unto all of Israel and to Joshua. He reminded them of what God had already done for them and that it was the Lord who would work on their behalf. He encouraged them; emphasizing that the Lord was the one who was going to go before them and be with them. *(Deuteronomy 31:1-2).*

Memory Verse *Deuteronomy 31:8* And the LORD, he it is that doth go before thee; he will be with thee, he will not fail thee, neither forsake thee: fear not, neither be dismayed.

Biblical Application

In order to possess the promised land Israel was going to have to fight some battles. Things were going to be tough at times. The people of the land seemed larger and stronger than Israel. Based on the evil report of the majority that had spied out the land; Israel was ready to return back to Egypt. Looking at the task ahead with the natural and logical mind, it seemed impossible. However, the most important factor was that the Lord was with them and he would ensure their victory. Based upon His promises, there was no need to fear the people of the promised land. They were bread for them and their defense had departed from them (Num 14:9). During difficult times in this life, we must recall to our mind that the Lord is with us and he will not fail nor forsake us.

- The Lord is with us. *Deuteronomy 31:1-8; Genesis 28:13-15; Joshua 1:5, 9; I Chronicles 28:20; Hebrews 13:5.*

- Sihon and Og were proof of the Lord's faithfulness. *Deuteronomy 31: 4; Numbers 21: 21-35; Joshua 2:10-11.*

- The consequences of sin. *Joshua 6: 3-12; Isaiah 59: 1-15.*

- He abideth faithful. *Deuteronomy 7:9-24; II Timothy 2:13; Numbers 23:19; Luke 1:37.*

Everyday Life Application

What habits have you developed to help you refocus on the promises of God during the difficulties of life?

PURITY ON THE INSIDE

Introduction

Purity, according to the Webster's Dictionary, is the quality or state of being pure, which is simply being free from dust, dirt or taint. Our Lord and Savior throughout the gospels (*Matthew 23*) taught extensively on this subject. Although external cleanliness has its place, Jesus did not only teach from this perspective, but he also emphasized cleansing on the inside. Internal cleansing adjust one's thoughts, desires, feelings, and motives submitted to the will and word of God.

Memory Verse *Galatians 5:24* And they that are Christ's have crucified the flesh with the affections and lusts.

Biblical Application

When we accept Jesus as Lord, and receive his spirit, then we possess the power to overcome. We play a major role in our own purity for there are many New Testament Scriptures that exhort us to purge and/or cleanse ourselves; moving beyond external behavior, to a change of heart. We are to crucify our flesh, by submitting to the written Word, and yielding to the Spirit's leading. The Holy Scripture reminds us that God looks upon the heart *(I Samuel 16:7)*. The objective and goal is to be like Christ inside and out, to have this testimony that Satan has nothing in us *(John 14:30)*. Ultimately, we want to please God and make ready for his return.

- Jesus focused on the internal. *Matthew 5:27-28, 23:25-28.*

- The part we play in cleansing. *Romans 12:1-2; Colossians 3: 4-*

  10; II Corinthians: 6:15-18, 7:1, 10:3-6; I John 3:2-3.

- Our examples to follow. *I Corinthians 9:27; John 14:30.*

Everyday Life Application

List and discuss possible strategies to achieve internal purity.

Discuss strategies already being implemented.

Author: *Elder James Taylor, Jr.*

REBUKE

Introduction

Paul, in his wisdom, taught Timothy and Titus how to develop into strong leaders for the church. Paul was a man of great wisdom, strength, and boldness. He is credited as a person who even called out the Apostle Peter rightly. Strong leadership is one that must embrace all aspects. An important and critical task of leadership is to correct those who need to be corrected.

Memory Verse *Galatians 2:11* "But when Peter was come to Antioch, I withstood him to the face, because he was to be blamed".

Biblical Application

We learn a lot about relationships in the sacred text. Important aspects of relationships that must not be forgotten, is rebuke and accountability. Those closest to you are those who can identify your errors and present them to you. We all need that. We need people who love us enough to guide us back unto the right path when we slip or willfully err. We need people who are not afraid of how we feel and can tell us the truth.[9]

- The truth spoken is the love in some cases. *Proverbs 27:5.*
- Good questions from those who care make you think about your next move. *Genesis 4:6-7.*
- We cannot be afraid of conflict and feelings. *Galatians 2:1-21.*

---

[9] https://www.psychologytoday.com/us/blog/how-we-work/201601/the-right-way-hold-people-accountable

- Rebuke with patience, teaching and forgiving heart. 2 Timothy 4:2, Luke 17:3.

Everyday Life Application

Hebrews chapter 12 details the plight of a bastard, as one without anyone to correct them. The text says it is something that is good for all of us. Think about the last time this important part of life, correction happened to you. How did you respond? Was it in terror, was it in disbelief, was it in anger, was it in gratitude? Discuss the benefits of this level of truth.

Author: *Elder David T. Brand Jr. MA, LPC*

BE STRONG AND VERY COURAGEOUS

Introduction

The book of Joshua begins with the Lord commanding Joshua to go with the children of Israel over the Jordan River to possess the land the Lord promised to them. Taking possession of the land was no small task. It would require miraculous interventions from the Lord and great faith from the people. In three out of nine verses of chapter 1, the Lord reiterated his encouragement to Joshua to be strong and of good courage and not to be afraid or dismayed.

Memory Verse *Joshua 1:7* Only be thou strong and very courageous, that thou mayest observe to do according to all the law, which Moses my servant commanded thee: turn not from it to the right hand or to the left, that thou mayest prosper whithersoever thou goest.

Biblical Application

The strength and courage referred to in *Joshua 1* are not physical. Although the people needed to fight to possess the land, the exhortation is referring to maintaining spiritual focus and obedience to the law of God. Strength in this context means to fasten; to seize, and courage is defined as being alert physically or mentally. (Strong's Dictionary). Joshua had to stay alert and fastened to the law of God; not turning to the right hand or to the left hand. The land was full of distractions and people that worshipped false gods. Today we are surrounded by a society that bows down to everything, except the true and living God. In order to maintain focus, God told Joshua to meditate day and night and not to stop talking about God's law.

Before his death, Joshua exhorted the people with the same word God had given him. Being strong and courageous enough not to turn aside from God's law is a result of our love for God. Let us take good heed unto ourselves that we love the Lord and cleave unto him. We must be strong and courageous to enter in at the straight gate; straight is the gate and narrow is the way which leadeth unto life, and few there be that find it.

- The Lord's exhortation to Joshua. *Joshua 1:1-9.*

- Meditate on God's law every day. *Psalm 119:97-104.*

- Joshua reiterated the word of the Lord. *Joshua 23: 1-16.*

- Obedience to the word is a result of love for God. *Psalm 40:8; John 14:15; I John 5:3; II John 1:6, Mat7:13-14.*

Everyday Life Application

What are some distractions that cause you to turn to the right hand or to the left of God's law?

Do you set aside time every day to read God's word and pray?

PRIDE GOETH BEFORE DESTRUCTION

Introduction

Social media provides a platform for self-promotion that was previously available to sports stars and actors only through television. Today, adults and children alike are pressured into a competitive social paradigm where we try to keep up with or outperform others. Some people gain an exaggerated sense of arrogance and pride based on their success in life or popularity received through social media. It is imperative that we keep our accomplishments in this life in proper perspective. "For promotion cometh neither from the east, nor from the west, nor from the south. But God is the judge: he putteth down one, and setteth up another" (Psalm 75:6-7).

Memory Verse *Proverbs 16:18* Pride goeth before destruction, and an haughty spirit before a fall.

Biblical Application

The Lord allowed Nebuchadnezzar king of Babylon to besiege Jerusalem. The king had great power and influence only because the Almighty allowed it. However, he had issues with anger and pride. Even after seeing the fourth person in the fiery furnace and acknowledging he was like the Son of God; he refused to humble himself. Nebuchadnezzar refused to acknowledge that "the Most High ruleth in the kingdom of men and giveth it to whomsoever he will". Instead the king stated that he had built the great Babylon by the might of his power and for the honor of his majesty. As the Lord allows us to accomplish our dreams in this life, we must maintain humility and give God the glory for our accomplishments

- Nebuchadnezzar refuses to truly repent. *Daniel 3:1-30.*

- The consequences of pride. *Daniel 4:18-33, 5:17-23; I Samuel 2:7; Psalm 10:2-6, 75:5-7; Proverbs 16:18-19, 18:12, 11:2.*
- Humility is paramount in our relationship the Lord. *Daniel 4:34-37; Micah 6:6-8; Luke 14:7-11; James 4:5-10; I Peter 5:5-7.*

Everyday Life Application

How can we give the glory to God for the things he enables us to accomplish?

What is the difference between pride and self-esteem?

SPEAK MY WORD FAITHFULLY

Introduction

There are a multitude of voices today who claim to speak the Word of God. The title prophet or prophetess is utilized widely. Many use verses and partial verses from the Bible in theatrical sermons to touch emotions and extort money for filthy lucre. Others fail to condemn sin and unrighteousness and overlook things that contradict the Word of God. Common prophesies heard today are for nonspecific blessings for the congregation or individuals. People often gather in great numbers to hear a "word from the Lord" from alleged prophets. Some replace a relationship with Christ and dedicated study of his written Word with hearing from a prophet. The Biblical examples of prophets are different from prophets seen today. They were frequently called to speak boldly about specific judgments that God was going to bring for sin.

Memory Verse *Jeremiah 23:28* The prophet that hath a dream, let him tell a dream; and he that hath my word, let him speak my word faithfully. What is the chaff to the wheat? saith the LORD.

Biblical Application

Jeremiah prophesied of the future judgment of God for sin. He proclaimed an unpopular message to rebellious people. He said that the whole land would be a desolation and an astonishment and that nations would serve the king of Babylon for seventy years. False prophets came with contradictory messages they claimed to be the word of the Lord. Some thought they could resist or fight the coming judgment. King Zedekiah sent Pashur and Zephaniah to get Jeremiah to inquire of the Lord. The word of the Lord to Jeremiah was that the way of life was to go out and fall to the siege of the Chaldeans. This meant submitting to the plan of the Lord. This was contrary to the message of the false prophets and not what people wanted to hear. Many today have itching ears and are seeking prophets and teachers who tell them things that are pleasant to their ears. Prophets that stand in the counsel of God will cause people to hear his words and turn from their evil way and from the evil of their doings.

- God's impending judgment. *Jeremiah 19:1-15, 20:1-6, 21:1-14, 25:1-11.*

- Profane priests and prophets. *Jeremiah 23:9-32, 28:1-17; Ezekiel 22:23-31.*

- Is there light in them? *Isaiah 8:16-22; Deuteronomy 13:1-5, 18:20-22; Nehemiah 9:26,30; II Timothy 4:2-5.*

Everyday Life Application

How can you avoid being deceived by a false prophet?

Did the role and or definition of the prophet change in the New Testament church?

What does it mean to preach the word in season and out of season?

A COVENANT WITH MINE EYES

Introduction

In our capitalistic society we are bombarded with marketing techniques on a daily basis. Through television, internet, and billboards we encounter advertisements that influence our behavior and decisions. Marketing is very effective at appealing to things that bring pleasure. From the time we are young, tremendous influence is placed on us to focus on the external appearance. We are encouraged to think that our outward appearance must be without blemish and a certain shape. Men and women alike go to great lengths to meet expectations for perfect physical appearance. This includes using the naked physical body to sell products or gain attention. As followers of Christ we must avoid partaking of the lusts of the flesh that are so prevalent in society.

Memory Verse *Job 31:1* I made a covenant with mine eyes; why then should I think upon a maid?

Biblical Application

The Lord described his servant Job as a perfect and an upright man, one that feared God and eschewed evil. One of the reasons Job maintained this relationship with God was the covenant he made with his eyes. He had made a decision not to think lustful thoughts about women he saw. Jesus warned of this temptation and declared that doing so was committing adultery in your heart. The sin David committed with Bathsheba began after he saw her washing herself on the rooftop and lusted after her. The Bible provides various warnings against sexual sins that apply to men and women alike. This includes guidance in the way we dress. If you are struggling with the sexual sins of lust, find a trusted prayer partner who can help you to overcome. Avoid entertaining lustful thoughts by casting down these imaginations and replacing them with other thoughts. It is also important to avoid placing yourself in tempting situations.

- Avoid lusting in your heart. *II Samuel 11:2-5; Matthew 5:27-30.*
- Avoid the way to hell. *Proverbs 5:15-23; 6:23-35, 7:1-27; James 1:12-15.*
- Dress modestly. *Exodus 20:22-26; I Timothy 2:9-10, I Peter 3:1-7.*
- *Avoid hate, 1 John 3:15-17.*

Everyday Life Application

What are some things you can do as a single person to avoid sexual sins?

How can you avoid exposure to sexually explicit images on television or the internet?

THE WEIGHTIER MATTERS OF THE LAW

Introduction

We as Sabbath and Feast day observers can sometimes be harsh in our approach to those who do not worship in our manner. Christ clearly lets us know that if we love him, we will keep his commandments, therefore being a Sabbath and Feast day observer is still relevant. However, as baptized believers we cannot hang the totality of our salvation on Sabbath and Feast day observance. God is looking for a weightier expression of our love for him.

Memory Verse *Matthew 23:23* Woe unto you, scribes and Pharisees, hypocrites! for ye pay tithe of mint and anise and cumin, and have omitted the weightier matters of the law, judgment, mercy, and faith: these ought ye to have done, and not to leave the other undone.

Biblical Application

In (*Matthew 22: 37-40)* Jesus was asked by a pharisees lawyer, what was the great commandment, Jesus did not respond with keep the feast days and Sabbath, but rather said unto him, Thou shalt love the Lord thy God with all thy heart, and with all thy soul, and with all thy mind. This was the first and great commandment. And the second was like unto it, Thou shalt love thy neighbor as thyself. On those two commandments hung all the law and the prophets. *James 2: 8-10* reminds us, "If ye fulfil the royal law according to the scripture, Thou shalt love thy neighbor as thyself, ye do well: But if ye have respect to persons, ye commit sin, and are convinced of the law as transgressors.". For whosoever shall keep the whole law, and yet offend in one point, he is guilty of all. Jesus in his interaction with the religious elite of his day was always at odds with them because of their lack of judgement, mercy and faith. For this reason, as believers, we must be cautious not to overlook the sins men can't see; the ones that go to the true heart of men.

- Judgment (justice). *Proverbs 21: 2-3; Proverbs 6:16-19; Matthew 5:22; James 3:1-18, Romans 13:8-11.*
- Mercy. *Micah 6:6-8, Hosea 6:6; Zachariah 7:9-10; Proverbs 3:3-4, 14:21, 21:13, 21:21; Luke: 6:36.*
- Faith. *Hebrews 11:6; John 3: 14-20; Provers 3:5-8.*

Everyday Life Application

Examining yourself which of these (Judgement, Mercy, and Faith) have you perfected and which do you need to work on?

Author: Evangelist Patricia Powell

PUT OFF ALL THESE

Introduction

What are you passionate about in this life? Are you highly motivated about a job or a specific career path? Perhaps you are a fierce competitor in sports or the arts. Sometimes our motivation to be the best we can be or to have things a certain way can cause emotions to arise that cause us to lose our focus on the Lord. Strong emotions sometimes cause us to react and do or say things we later regret. We must walk in the Spirit daily in order to keep our passion and emotions in subjection to the Word of God.

Memory Verse *Colossians 3:8-10* But now ye also put off all these; anger, wrath, malice, blasphemy, filthy communication out of your mouth. Lie not one to another, seeing that ye have put off the old man with his deeds; And have put on the new man, which is renewed in knowledge after the image of him that created him:

Biblical Application

Naaman was the captain of the army of the king of Syria. He was highly respected and honored. Described as a mighty man of valor, he was gifted and very good at what he did. His success caused him to be self-confident and proud. Naaman wanted to be healed from his leprosy and went to see the prophet Elisha. He became angry and left in a rage after Elisha instructed him to wash in the Jordan River seven times. The Jordan was known to be a muddy river and there were cleaner rivers in Damascus [10](Unger). Naaman was used to being successful by doing things his way. He had expectations of what the prophet should do in order for him to be healed. Sometimes the Lord leads us in ways that we don't expect or desire. Naaman expected to get some of the glory by accomplishing a great thing in the process of his healing. Let us be careful not to become so overly self-reliant and independent that we refuse to obey the Lord. Fortunately, Naaman listened to the counsel of his servants. He repented, obeyed, was healed, and later expressed faith in the Lord.

- Naaman almost missed his healing. *II Kings 5:1-14.*
- Put off the old man. *Ephesians 4:22-32; Colossians 3:8-10.*
- The Word of God exposes our emotions and discerns our thoughts and intents. *Hebrews 4:12-13.*
- God's ways are not our ways. *Isaiah 55:6-13.*

Everyday Life Application

What are some specific techniques you use to control your emotions?

How can you recognize and overcome triggers to your strong emotions?

What can you do daily to help ensure that you walk in the Spirit?

---

[10] Unger, M.F. (1988). The New Unger's Bible Dictionary. Moody Press, Chicago.

UNITY OF THE FAITH

Introduction

Unity is sometimes misunderstood as uniformity. God's people have always been composed of diverse people. Exodus 1 provides the names of the children of Israel that came into Egypt with Jacob and their households. Seventy souls came out of the loins of Jacob. In Egypt they were fruitful, increased abundantly, and multiplied to the number of 600,000 men when they came out. The body of Christ is made up people from various backgrounds, cultures, and locations. However, we should have one primary focus on Jesus Christ. Our mission to go and teach all nations will be more effective if we are unified. God so loved the world that he gave his only begotten Son; without discrimination, Scripture further states whosoever believeth on him should not perish but have everlasting life. The invitation is to all; whosoever shall call upon the name of the Lord shall be saved and whosoever will let him come and take the water of life freely.

Memory Verse *Ephesians 4:13* Till we all come in the unity of the faith, and of the knowledge of the Son of God, unto a perfect man, unto the measure of the stature of the fullness of Christ:

Biblical Application

Paul beseeched believers in Ephesians 4 to walk worthy of their vocation (invitation), maintaining all lowliness, meekness, longsuffering, and forbearing one another in love. Walking in love and maintaining these character traits is necessary in our endeavor to keep the unity of the Spirit. Unity in *Ephesians 4* is defined as oneness (Strong's Dictionary). Jesus prayed in John 17 that we would be one. One is the root word from which unity is derived. Jesus prayed that we would be one, so that the world would believe. The gifts of the fivefold ministry (Eph 4:11), were given for the perfecting of the saints, the work of the ministry and to edify the body of Christ. The goal of the ministry is to come in the unity of the faith. Unity of the faith is necessary along with the knowledge of the Son of God in order to come unto a perfect man and reach the measure of the stature of the fullness of Christ. However, it seems that the desire for titles and positions is sometimes used to split churches. This is evident by those who gain titles and followers and leave the church to start their own new organizations over insignificant differences. Instead of walking in lowliness and meekness; forbearing one another in love and focusing on one Lord, one faith, and one baptism, many have allowed pride to cause division. Let us avoid being carnal and following fleshly desires. Instead, we should endeavor to keep the unity of the Spirit in the bond of peace.

- Israel was diverse. *Exodus 1:1-7, 12:37-38, 48-49.*
- Endeavor to keep the unity of the Spirit. *Ephesians 4:1-16, Psalm 133:1-3.*
- Jesus prayed that we would be one. *John 17:20-23.*
- Avoid being carnal. *I Corinthians 1:1-17, 3:1-11; Proverbs 6:16-19.*

Everyday Life Application

How can we allow the Lord to work in us to build the unity of the faith? What does it mean to sow discord amongst the brethren?

PASSOVER AND FEAST OF UNLEAVENED BREAD

Introduction

In *Genesis 15*, God told Abraham that his seed would serve and be afflicted as strangers in a land for 400 years. The children of Israel were made to serve with rigor, in bondage and affliction in Egypt. The Lord instructed Moses to tell Pharaoh to let his people go so that they could hold a feast to him in the wilderness. God told Moses that Pharaoh would not let them go, until he had stretched out his arm and smote them with all his wonders. The Lord purposely raised up Pharaoh to show in him his power and so that his name would be declared though out all the earth. This was all part of the Lord's plan to exercise judgment against the gods of Egypt and deliver Israel through the institution of the Lord's Passover.

Memory Verse *Exodus 12:13* And the blood shall be to you for a token upon the houses where ye are: and when I see the blood, I will pass over you, and the plague shall not be upon you to destroy you, when I smite the land of Egypt.

Biblical Application

The Lord gave specific instructions regarding the first observance of Passover. Details provided were important because the Lord's Passover was about much more than deliverance from Egypt after 430 years. The Passover lamb pointed to a much greater deliverance from bondage that would occur hundreds of years later. At the first Passover, they were unaware of the future significance of the lamb. The bible declares; "...the prophets have enquired and searched diligently,... searching what, or what manner of time the Spirit of Christ in them did signify, when it testified beforehand the sufferings of Christ, and the glory that should follow."(1Pet 1:10-11). As Jesus celebrated Passover with his disciples, he blessed the bread and gave thanks for the cup and shared with them. He declared the bread was his body and the cup was his blood of the New Testament; shed for many for the remission of sins. The disciples still did not have the revelation of the significance of what Jesus said even up to the point that he met them on the road to Emmaus. Oh, what a blessing that we have the Scriptures and the Spirit of God to reveal unto us the mystery of Christ that was previously not made known to the sons of men. The Lamb of God, Jesus Christ our Passover shed his blood and suffered a horrible death so that all who believe and call upon the name of the Lord could be saved.

- The Lamb was the Lord's Passover. *Exodus 12:1-17; Leviticus 23:4-8.*
- Jesus' blood of the new testament. *Matthew 26:17-75; Luke 22:1-71.*
- The mystery of Christ revealed. *Mark 9:30-32; Luke 10:23-24, 18:31-34; John 12:16 Ephesians 3:1-5; Romans 16:25-26; Colossians 1:26-27.*
- Hear, believe, call and be delivered. *Romans 10:5-21.*

Everyday Life Application

How has the revelation of the Lamb of God brought you out of bondage? How can you express your gratitude for the what Jesus has done for you personally?

THE FEAST OF UNLEAVENED BREAD

Introduction

We rejoice and celebrate the Lord's Feast in obedience to the Scriptures. This is a special time of year in churches and families around the world. Traditions regarding eating unleavened bread are enjoyed by many. The love and fellowship of the saints during this time is strong and edifying. Observance of this feast brings joy and thanksgiving as we are about our Father's business.

Memory Verse *Mark 14:36* And he said, Abba, Father, all things are possible unto thee; take away this cup from me: nevertheless, not what I will, but what thou wilt,

Biblical Application

Mary had been visited by the angel Gabriel and told that the Holy Ghost would come upon her and power of the Highest would overshadow her. Joseph was visited by the angel of the Lord and told she conceived by the Holy Ghost; but they still didn't fully understand the mission of Jesus Christ. During his life on earth as the son of man, Jesus was always about his Father's business. His prayer life, miracles, and teaching were all the Father's will. In his most difficult and stressful time, he asked his disciples to watch as he prayed. Jesus asked the Father three times if his cup of suffering could pass, but his conclusion is what mattered the most. His conclusion was the same commitment that guided his entire sinless life; nevertheless, not my will but thine be done. May we dedicate ourselves to live our lives in total submission to the will of the Father.

- Keep the Feast. *Exodus 23:14-17, 34:18; Deuteronomy 16:1-8.*
- The Father's business. *Luke 2:41-52; John 5:15-47.*

- Nevertheless, not as I will, but as thou will. *Matthew 6:10, 26:36-46.*

Everyday Life Application

As we celebrate the Lord's Feast what are some specific things, you can do to be about your Father's business? What are some things you need to eliminate that are not about your Father's business? The family of Jesus went up to Jerusalem every year at the Feast of Passover/Unleavened Bread. When Jesus was a 12-year-old child, he was found missing from the caravan of people headed home after the feast. After three days of searching and much distress; his parents found him in the temple teaching others about the Father.

EXERCISE THE NAME OF JESUS

Introduction

To call upon the Lord for help is an act of faith and is always a good thing. But our Lord also gave us the ability to use his name when many types of circumstances arise. As believers of Jesus, it's time for us to exercise faith, and begin to speak to situations, and circumstances, in his name. It is not suggested that every time we use the name of Jesus, we get the desired results, but rather that every time we use His name the miraculous is always possible.

Memory Verse *James 5:14* Is any sick among you? Let him call for the elders of the church and let them pray over him, anointing him with oil in the name of the Lord.

Biblical Application

After his resurrection, Jesus declared that all power is given unto him in heaven and in earth (*Matthew 28:18*). As a result, the name of Jesus, is a name above every name *(Philippians 2:9)* Everything is subject to the name. Not only that, but we have baptism, we receive salvation, we obtain healing and deliverance, in the name. The word "name' in Strong's Concordance, is ŏnŏma, which simply means authority. Simply put, it's Jesus's authority that can and will produce results. We, as believers, have the ability to exercise this authority. This authority is not accessible by the unbeliever; the scripture teaches that such attempts can have catastrophic results (*Acts 19: 13-16*). But for the believer, it is a weapon to bring change, not only to the church, but to a lost and dying world.

- Signs for the believer. *Mark 16: 15-18.*
- Devils are subject. *Luke 10:17; Mark 9: 38-39.*

- Miracles in the Name. *Acts 3:6-8, 16; James 5:14-15; Acts 9:33-34.*
- Miracles while preaching the Name. *Acts 8: 5-7, 10:34-44.*
- Producing results, using His name. *Romans 10:8-13*

Everyday Life Application

Find documented miracles in history outside the Scriptures.

Testify to miracles, either witnessed, or performed in His name.

Author: *Elder James Taylor, Jr.*

IT'S COMING

Introduction

What's coming!? It is the judgment and wrath of God upon the wicked of this present evil world. It's called the *"The Great Day of the Lord"* or the *"Day of His Vengeance"* as described in Scripture. Although many would rather this not be a reality; choosing to steer clear of the conversation all together. While others would prefer to believe that God's wrath is not real; insisting such a thing would be a blemish on the character of God. Yet, God makes it plain, He will deal with the unrepentant and the rebellious *"...who know not God and on those who do not obey the gospel..."* II Thessalonians 1:8.

Memory Verse *Luke 3:7* Then said he to the multitude that came forth to be baptized of him, O generation of vipers, who hath warned you to flee from the wrath to come?

Biblical Application

For those in denial of how God feels about wickedness, they only have but to search the scriptures. The first world; in the days of Noah was so full of violence and wickedness; God's wrath was kindled and He destroyed the world with a flood, saving only a single family. The cities of Sodom and Gomorrah were so wicked, that only a single family was saved, as God destroyed those cities by fire from heaven. Israel upon entering the promised land was used by God as a rod of judgment to destroy the surrounding nations because of their abominations in the land. However, in each case mentioned above we see God extending mercy and salvation to the righteous by faith; as with Noah, Lot, and Rahab. This lesson serves as a reminder for us to be ready to escape the soon coming judgment and meet the King in peace.

- Judgment of God. *Deuteronomy 18:9-13; Luke 17:26-30; II Thessalonians 1:3-10.*
- An escape. *Luke 21:25-36; Hebrews 2:1-3; I Thessalonians 1:8-10.*

Everyday Life Application

What's most important in preparing to meet the King in peace?

Author: *Minister Robert O. Johnson*

BLESSED ARE THE POOR IN SPIRIT

Introduction

What did it take for you to realize your need for salvation through Jesus Christ? For some of us, it took extreme circumstances for us to submit to Christ. This may have been financial difficulties, health problems, or family issues. Becoming poor in spirit involves us reaching a point where we acknowledge we are spiritually poor(beggars) and bankrupt; dependent upon Christ for deliverance (Strong's Dictionary).

Memory Verse *Matthew 5:3 Blessed are the poor in spirit: for theirs is the kingdom of heaven.*

Biblical Application

David tried to cover his sin of adultery with Bathsheba by tricking her husband Uriah into thinking the child she conceived was his. After Uriah refused to sleep in his house, David had him killed in battle. God used Nathan the prophet to expose his sins. He pronounced the judgment of death upon the child that was born to them. David besought the Lord and fasted seven days; however, the child still died. David wrote *Psalm 51* in repentance for his sins. He came to realize firsthand that the sacrifices of God are a broken spirit: a broken and contrite heart, O God thou will not despise.

- Judgment and repentance. *II Samuel 12:1-20. Psalm 51:1-17, 34:18.*
- The Lord found us polluted in our own blood. *Ezekiel 16:1-13.*
- Save me, O God. *Psalm 69:1-36.*
- Don't forget after being delivered. *Deuteronomy 6:10-15, 8:1-20.*

Everyday Life Application

Does being poor in spirit occur only once in the life of a believer? How can you maintain this state in your relationship with Christ?

WHEN WE SUPPORT GOD'S HOUSE

Introduction

From the days of old, God set up a system whereby his house would have the provision needed to maintain its operations. When the Apostles set order for the church; likewise, a system was set up that provision would be made for those in the church. We are now in the 21st Century and the church stills needs the assistance of the congregants to maintain the operation of the church.

Memory Verse *Malachi 3:10* Bring ye all the tithes into the storehouse, that there may be meat in mine house, and prove me now herewith, saith the LORD of hosts, if I will not open you the windows of heaven, and pour you out a blessing, that there shall not be room enough to receive it**.**

Biblical Application

In *Exodus 36,* the chapter after God had given Moses the design for the tabernacles. It becomes obvious that the Tabernacle was not to be a shabby dwelling made of the cheapest materials one could find. No, this was the place God's presence would be and thus it was to be suited for a God. In order to provide the resources needed the people were commanded to contribute their resources i.e. their gold, silver, and their materials. The people gave to the point they had given more than enough for the task and were told to cease their giving. In addition, He put his Spirit on different individuals to do wood work, the art of tapestry, etc. The care of God's house not only finds precedence in the Old Testament Scriptures, but the New Testament as well. Just like in the days of old, God is still anointing people for service in the church: teachers, singers, musicians, business administrators, organizer etc.; all to benefit the up building of the kingdom. God has made promises to his people when we support his house. *Malachi 3: 8-12* is a clear promise that he would open up the window of heaven and pour out a blessing that there would not be room enough to be received. When we take care of God's house, He will take care of yours.

- A willing Spirit. *Exodus 35: 4-29; I Chronicles 29:1-14.*
- God loves a Cheerful giver. *II Corinthians 9: 1-7.*
- God gives the ability to work in his service. *Exodus 31: 1-11; Acts 6:1-3; Ephesians 4: 11-16.*
- God's promises when you give. *Proverbs 3: 9-10, 11:25; Malachi 3: 10-12; II Corinthian 9: 8-10.*
- We must be good stewards of God's house. *Genesis 39: 1-6; Luke 12: 42-48.*

Everyday Life Application

Getting out of the message of salvation through Jesus Christ is more crucial than ever. What talent and resources has God blessed you with to aide this process?

Author: *Evangelist Patricia Powell*

JESUS, CREATOR OF THE UNIVERSE

Introduction

In Merriam Webster, creator is defined as one that creates, usually by bringing something new or original into being, capitalizing the first letter of the reference "God".   The Greek translators of the Old Testament chose to use the Greek word *ektisen* in place of the Hebrew *qoneh*. *Ektisen* means "He created." According to Scripture, Jesus is the Creator of the universe. Scripture shows that the second person of the Godhead, Jesus, did the actual work of creation. Those who deny the deity of Christ will often say that he never claimed to be divine, and that his divinity is something that was ascribed to him later by the early church. This is not historically accurate. Not only did Jesus claim to be divine in a variety of different ways during his earthly ministry, he claimed to be the creator of the universe specifically.

Memory Verse: *Colossians 1:14-19.* Who is the image of the invisible God, the firstborn of every creature: For by him were all things created, that are in heaven, and that are in earth, visible and invisible, whether they be thrones, or dominions, or principalities, or powers: all things were created by him, and for him:

Biblical Application

In Scripture, Jesus said He was God (*John 10:33*). He proclaimed His existence before Abraham (*John 8:58*). Jesus proclaimed to be the "I Am" that existed prior to Abraham, and Jesus believed himself to be the creator of the universe. Jesus proclaimed Himself to be Yahweh. And Yahweh proclaimed to have created the universe by Himself (*Isaiah 44:24).* We could look at verses where he claimed to be the

Messiah and the fulfillment of prophecy, or verses where he claimed to have attributes and authority only God had. Throughout Scripture, Jesus claimed to be the Son of Man. "Son of Man" refers to a figure that Jews recognized as having divine authority. Read what the Jewish prophet Daniel wrote in *Daniel 7:13-14*. Jesus claimed to be the Divine Messiah *(Mark 14:60-64.)* He claimed to forgive sins *(Mark 2:1-12)*. He claimed to be Lord of the Sabbath *(Mark 2:28)*.

- God is before all things. *Colossians 1:17; Psalm 90:2.*
- God Produced all things. *Genesis 1:1;* Colossians 1:16.
- God sustains all things. *Hebrews 1:1-3.*
- God owns all things. *Psalm 24:1-2; I Chronicles 29:14.*

Everyday Life Application

In today's society, discuss the relevancy and importance of knowing God *(Jesus)* as Creator of heaven and earth.

Author: *Evangelist Irene Crawford*

MADE THEM MALE AND FEMALE

Introduction

The Lord created man from the dust of the earth and breathed into his nostrils the breath of life. After putting him in the garden of Eden, God said that it was not good that the man should be alone. He took one of Adam's ribs and made a woman. The Lord God then brought the woman to the man. The Bible declares that a man shall leave his father and mother; shall cleave unto his wife and they shall be one flesh. God created man in his own image, in the image of God created he him; male and female created he them. And God blessed them, and God said unto them, be fruitful, and multiply, and replenish the earth, and subdue it: and have dominion over the fish of the sea, and over the fowl of the air, and over every living thing that moveth upon the earth.

Memory Verse *Matthew 19:4* And he answered and said unto them, Have ye not read, that he which made them at the beginning made them male and female.

Biblical Application

The Scriptures are clear that the Lord's plan from the beginning for marriage was one man and one woman. The command to be fruitful and multiply can only be accomplished by a male and female. Modern man has gone to great efforts to distort the original plan of God. Widespread efforts to redefine marriage have been written into law in many countries. These efforts have also been accepted by some church denominations who claim to believe the Bible. Some parents are allowing or encouraging their children to attempt to change their gender by taking hormones and wearing clothes of the opposite sex. Many of the sexual sins accepted by society today are defined as abominations in the Bible.

- Male and female created He them. *Genesis 1:27-28, 2:15,18,21-25*
- Jesus confirms the original plan. *Matthew 19:3-12.*
- Abominations defined. *Leviticus 18:1-30; 20:7-22; Deuteronomy 22:5; Romans 1: 18-32; I Corinthians 6:9-10, 15-20.*

Everyday Life Application

How can we avoid allowing society teach our children that what the Lord calls an abomination is acceptable?

DAY OF PENTECOST

Introduction

After his crucifixion, Jesus spent three days and three nights in the grave in fulfillment of the prophecy of Jonah. Christ was then resurrected from the dead and shewed himself alive after his passion by many infallible proofs. He was seen of the apostles for forty days and spoke of the things pertaining to the kingdom of God. Jesus commanded them that they should not depart from Jerusalem, but wait for the promise of the Father. This promise would be the fulfillment of his word; when he said John truly baptized with water; but ye shall be baptized with the Holy Ghost not many days hence.

Memory Verse *Acts 1:8* But ye shall receive power, after that the Holy Ghost is come upon you: and ye shall be witnesses unto me both in Jerusalem, and in all Judaea, and in Samaria, and unto the uttermost part of the earth.

Biblical Application

Prior to the ascension of Jesus back into heaven, he told his disciples they would receive power after that Holy Ghost had come upon them. This power would enable them to be witnesses unto him to the uttermost part of the earth. The disciples remained in Jerusalem and continued on one accord with prayer and supplication. When the day of Pentecost was fully come or fulfilled (Thayer's Dictionary) the Holy Ghost sat upon them in the upper room. They spoke the wonderful works of God in other tongues. Other tongues which were the native languages of the multitude from every nation that had gathered at Jerusalem for Pentecost. When these devout men came to see the move of God, they were amazed and confounded because they each heard their native language. The Holy Ghost speaks today to people from every kindred, tongue, and nation. He knows every language and every heart. There is no speech nor language where the voice of God is not heard through his creation. Today God still uses the Holy Ghost to speak through witnesses to the uttermost part of the earth. The Holy Ghost speaks the wonderful works of God to every language of people throughout the world. While the body of Christ may emphasize the Holy Ghost through speaking in unknown tongues; the Scripture also bears witness to him speaking in each individuals' known tongue, meeting them where they are. The Apostle Paul stated that he spoke with tongues more than many. However, at church he said he would rather speak five words with his understanding to teach others instead of 10,000 words in an unknown tongue. Let us allow the Holy Ghost to use us to be witnesses for Christ spreading the gospel of Jesus Christ to the lost. Pray for discernment and wisdom to be ready to share the love of Christ and speak the Word in season and out of season.

- The day of Pentecost fully came. *Acts 1:1-14, 2:1-47.*
- The Holy Ghost speaks. *I Corinthians 2:1-10; Psalm 19:1-4.*
- Witness with understanding, meekness, and love. *I Corinthians 14:1-20; Galatians 6:1-10; Matthew 28:16-20; Ephesians 4:11-16.*
- The Feast of Weeks. *Exodus 23:16-17; Deuteronomy 16:9-12.*

Everyday Life Application

How has the Holy Ghost used you to witness for Christ? What can you do to better allow yourself to be led by the Spirit of God to reach others for Jesus?

DISCOURAGEMENT

Introduction

One of the hardest concepts of this walk is that we must suffer if we are to reign with Christ one day. Disciples must have the discipline to endure. If you are not mentally and emotionally strong, the stretch will leave you very sore. Jesus mentioned bearing a cross, David mentioned the many afflictions of the righteous. We must endure hardness, we must overcome obstacles, we must go through and not around. We must be proven in the war of life. Discouragement is a natural occurrence when following Christ, and it does not equate to weakness. Discouragement has been seen in everyone from Adam, to Job, to David, to the prophets, to the apostles, and even Christ himself. Discouragement is not always a sign of weakness; it is often a sign of strength. It takes a strong person to cry. It takes a strong person to understand they need help. It takes courage and strength to bounce back, to see the light at the end of the proverbial tunnel, to believe God even when life presents severe obstacles and you feel completely left alone. Immanuel...God is with us.

Memory Verse *Psalm 42:3* My tears have been my meat day and night, while they continually say unto me, where is thy God?

Biblical Application

The truth of life is, hard situations happen, often. There are times when we have several bad choices to choose from. Spiritually, Christ said and did things the average person struggled to fully understand. The things He allows and ordains in our lives are out of our control and beyond our knowledge. We have the capacity to grow, to learn, to cope, and to be resilient. [11]Resilience is a good term to describe the ability to bounce back after adversity.

- The things Jesus said were sometimes hard to swallow. *John 6:60-67.*
- Some of the things Jesus allows in life are hard to process. *John 11:1-7.*
- The hardest parts are opportunities for growth! *II Corinthians 4:14-18.*
- Strength is birthed in courage. *II Samuel 12:15-23.*

Everyday Life Application

Resilience is a powerful skill to cultivate in life. It is the power to bounce back, to cope, to process, and move forward. Remember times when you were resilient, graciously share with others the tips and skills that got you through.

Author: *Elder David T. Brand Jr. MA, LPC*

---

[11] https://www.psychologytoday.com/us/blog/science-choice/202005/the-8-key-elements-resilience

DO MY STATUTES, YOU SHALL LIVE IN THEM

Introduction

Confusion exists among believers today about God's law. Most will agree certain commandments are valid such as "thou shalt not commit adultery" or "thou shalt not kill". However, most refuse to observe the Sabbath or Feasts of the Lord. People commonly say they are not "under the law" to justify not keeping the Lord's Sabbaths. Others who observe God's Law often fail to realize salvation is apart from works of the law. Many fail to rightly divide God's Word and often isolate verses out of context. Jesus said, think not that he had come to destroy the law or the prophets, he did not come to destroy but to fulfill. Paul wrote, wherefore the law is holy, and the commandment holy, and just, and good. The commandment was ordained to life, but because of sin he found it to be unto death. The primary problem was not with the law, but with our flesh and sin.

Memory Verse *Leviticus 18: 5* Ye shall therefore keep my statutes, and my judgments: which if a man do, he shall live in them: I am the LORD.

Biblical Application

Leviticus 18:5 is quoted in *Romans 10:5,* "For Moses describeth the righteousness which is of the law, that the man which doeth those things shall live by them". Righteousness through the law was based upon personal works of observing it without error. If a man do (work, accomplish, make) he shall live (have life, remain alive) in them (Brown Driver Briggs Lexicon). We have all sinned and broken God's law at some point in our lives. Examples of failure to obtain righteousness or live through the law are found in *Ezekiel 20:11-13,21* and *Nehemiah 9:28-29.* In *Romans 10,* Paul states how he wants Israel to be saved, but they have not accepted the righteousness of God through faith in Christ. The righteousness of God is obtained through faith in Christ; apart from works of the law. It is important to establish that we are saved by grace apart from works. However; the law is not made void through faith; we establish the law through faith. Our faith is made perfect through works. Even as Abraham was circumcised as a seal of the righteousness of the faith, he had being yet uncircumcised. For before being circumcised, Abraham believed God and it was counted to him for righteousness.

- If a man do, he shall live. *Nehemiah 9:28-29, Ezekiel 20: 11-13,21*
- All have transgressed the law. *Deuteronomy 11:26-28, 27:26; James 2:8-12; Romans 3:1-20.*
- Christ is the end of the law for righteousness. *Romans 9:30-33, 10:1-14; Galatians 3:1-24; Philippians 3:8-11.*

Everyday Life Application

How would you explain to others that keeping the commandments is not grievous? What are some of the blessings you enjoy by observing the Lord's Sabbaths?

GOD IS

Introduction

If a poll were taken with the question asked, who is God? One can only imagine the myriad of responses that would follow. Such as, God is a Supreme being, whoever he or she is. Or, God is a mysterious invisible force in the universe. For others, God is a transcendent being, indifferent to the plight and suffering of men. For some, God is non-existent, a fictitious being, made up as an opioid to help control the minds of the disenfranchised. Still for others, God is Nature or whatever they choose Him to be. Thankfully, God has graciously unveiled the truth of Himself in scripture. This lesson reminds us of the importance of knowing God personally.

Memory Verse *Psalm 118:14* The LORD is my strength and song and is become my salvation.

Biblical Application

To Noah, God is a God of "wrath" upon the wicked, yet a "preserver" of the righteous. For Abraham, God is a promise "keeper" who fulfills His word in His appointed time. For Daniel, God is "sovereign" changing the times and the seasons, removing kings, and setting up kings. For Moses, God is "merciful" and "longsuffering" in the face of Israel's unbelief and rebellion. For King Hezekiah, God is a "healer" from terminal illness. For Job, God is a "restorer of life and llessing" in the face of total loss. To Joshua, He is a God that "strengthens" for the battle, giving complete victory over all enemies. For Samson, He is a God of a "second chances" hearing the prayer of the righteous in times of distress.

- God proclaims His goodness. *Exodus 34:5-8.*

- Glorious in Power. *Exodus 15:1-11.*
- Our Rock and Salvation. *Psalm 62:1-8, 91:1-10.*

Everyday Life Application

Our world is filled with struggles and disappointments, which often brings us face to face with life's ultimate question. Who is God and who is He to us?

Author: *Minister Robert O. Johnson*

BLESSED ARE THE MEEK

Introduction

Meek in the *Matthew 5:5* is defined as mild or humble (Strong's Dictionary). Meekness is a part of Godly character that is often lacking in our society and among followers of Christ. The Scriptures warn us not to think of ourselves more highly than we ought to think but to think soberly as God hath dealt to every man the measure of faith. Our accomplishments in the church, in education, or in our careers are only a result of the grace of God in our lives. We should not strive for position or titles. Instead let us serve faithfully in the capacity assigned to us and wait for the Lord to open doors for us.

Memory Verse *Matthew 5:5* Blessed are the meek: for they shall inherit the earth.

Biblical Application

Moses was described as very meek, above all the men which were upon the face of the earth. In this context, Miriam and Aaron attempted an insurrection to usurp leadership over him. Moses had previously made mistakes in anger. In this situation, it may have been tempting for Moses to intervene on his own. Instead of acting hastily in anger, Moses interceded for God to heal Miriam. He then honored the Lord's decision and shut her out of camp for seven days. The Bible describes him as faithful in all his house as a servant. Despite his mistakes, overall, Moses directed the people to follow the Lord and allowed the Lord to maintain his headship, even after the Lord said he would not enter the promised land. It is important for us to be humble ourselves under the mighty hand of God, and be led by him in our relationship with him and others.

- Moses was meek and faithful. *Numbers 12:1-16; Hebrews 3:1-5.*

- Jesus was meek. *Matthew 11:28-30; II Corinthians 10:1.*
- Put on meekness. *Psalm 37:8-11, 25:8-10; Galatians 5:22-26; Ephesians 4:1-3; Colossians 3:12-13; I Timothy 6:11-12; James 3:13-18.*
- The servant of the Lord must not strive. *II Timothy 2:22-26.*

Everyday Life Application

How have you exhibited meekness in situations at church and work? Think about a situation in which you could have reacted differently and exhibited meekness. What will you change next time?

GOD'S PLAN OF SALVATION

Introduction

Merriam Webster defines Salvation as deliverance from the power and effects of sin. A plan is typically any diagram or list of steps with details of timing and resources, used to achieve an objective to do something. It is commonly understood as a temporal set of intended actions through which one expects to achieve a goal; a detailed proposal for doing or achieving something. Scripture reveals that God laid out His amazing purpose and plan for mankind *before* time began. Only the Bible, boldly claims there was a moment when time, as we know it, *did not exist.* The most important thing to understand about the plan of salvation is that it is God's plan; He owns it. In God's plan of salvation, God Himself is the only one who can provide for our salvation. We are utterly unable to save ourselves because of our sin and its consequences. God became a human being in the person of Jesus Christ (*John 1:1, 14*).

Memory Verse: *Ephesians 1:4* According as he hath chosen us in him before the foundation of the world, that we should be holy and without blame before him in love:

Biblical Application

Jesus Christ was the revelation, personification, and incarnation of God to men. In Christ, the plan is presented to men. Jesus lived a sinless life and offered Himself as a perfect sacrifice on our behalf. Since Jesus is God, His death was of infinite and eternal value. The death of Jesus Christ on the cross fully paid for the sins of the entire world. His resurrection from the dead demonstrated that His sacrifice was indeed sufficient and that salvation is now available. The Bible makes it abundantly clear that there is only one plan of salvation. In God's plan of salvation, first we must understand why we need to be saved. Simply put, we need to be saved because we have sinned. The Bible declares that everyone has sinned. God is holy and cannot allow sin to go unpunished. The punishment for sin is death *(Romans 6:23)* and eternal separation from God *(Revelation 20:11–15)*. Without God's plan of salvation, eternal death is the destiny of every human being.

- Salvation is impossible without the Lord. *Acts 4:12; John 14:6.*
- Eternal Purpose of God. *Ephesians 3:11.*
- God's plan of salvation. *John 3:16; Ephesians 2:8-9.*
- God's plan accomplished. II *Timothy 1:9.*

Everyday Life Application

Believe the Word of God. *Believe* in Jesus Christ. Have faith in God.

Author: *Evangelist Irene Crawford*

FOLLOW THE INSTRUCTIONS

Introduction

God is explicit in the instructions and commands He gives to His people to obey. Moses tells the children of Israel to "Listen" meaning to hear the decrees and laws, "Follow" them so you may live, and do not "Add" to what is commanded of you, and do not "Subtract" from them. Since the LORD is our Rock and His way is perfect, it would behoove us to obey His instructions and be blessed, rather than rebel and suffer the consequences of disobedience. This lesson reminds us that trust and obedience to God is essential in acquiring the blessings He has for His people. This lesson also reminds us, "Cursed is the man whose heart departs from following the LORD" *Jeremiah 17:5.*

Memory Verse *Psalm 32:8* I will instruct thee and teach thee in the way which thou shalt go: I will guide thee with mine eye.

Biblical Application

If we deviate from God's instructions whether out of anger, personal desire, impatience, or out of ignorance or outright rebellion, the outcome can be costly. Moses was instructed to speak to the rock, but out of his anger, he struck the rock twice, and lost out on entering the promise land. Solomon knew the command of God not to intermarry with anyone from the surrounding nations, but out of his own personal desires he married many strange women; Consequently, his kingdom was divided. King Saul was instructed to wait on the prophet Samuel to offer a sacrifice to the Lord, but in his impatience, he offered the sacrifice and the Kingdom was now taken from him. David, zealous for moving the Ark of the Covenant to Jerusalem, out of ignorance to the instructions of God on how it was to be moved, caused his servant Uzzah to lose his life. Aaron's sons received instruction on how to minister in the sanctuary, but out of rebellion they offered strange (unauthorized) fire and were destroyed.

- Defeat in Disobedience. *Numbers 14:35-45; Joshua 7:1-13.*
- Rebellion is a sin. *I Samuel 15:1-23.*
- Victory and blessing in obedience. *Judges 7:1-15, Deuteronomy 28:1-14; Jeremiah 17:20-27.*

Everyday Life Application

What blessings have you received in obedience to God?

Author: *Minister Robert O. Johnson*

THE FALSE PROPHET

Introduction

Throughout the scope of time, God has used men and women to be prophets. In the Old Testament, you had individuals like Moses, Deborah and Samuel. In the New Testament, you had people like Agabus and Phillip's daughters. The prophet's role, was, and is to be his spokesperson. To speak on His behalf, present and for future. Prophets according to Strong's Dictionary, is "4396 Prophetes, which means a foreteller, and also inspired speaker", who declares the heart of God. They are foretellers because they sometimes speak of events that will take place in the future. To be a prophet, one has to be placed in the office by God; it's not something one can choose to be. The role of the prophet is for the perfecting of the saints, for the work of the ministry, for the edifying of the body of Christ *(Ephesians 4:11-12)*. In essence to draw people to God. My brothers and sisters, anytime God does a work or establishes an order to something, Satan always has a counterfeit. In this lesson, the counterfeit is the false prophet to which the Bible gives clear warning against them.

Memory Verse *Matthew 7:15* Beware of false prophets, which come to you in sheep's clothing, but inward they are ravening wolves.

Biblical Application

Words such as spurious, pretend, imposter and illegitimate are associated with the term false prophet. Holman's Dictionary says, the false prophet is a person who spreads false messages and teachings, claiming to speak God's words. Unlike the true prophet, he is not ordained by God, but ordained by Satan or may be self-appointed, with an objective to divide and lead people away from the will and Word of God. Lack of godliness in lifestyle is also a trait of being false. Because of the mainstream appeal of ministry, and the celebration and popularity of today's prophets, and the monetary revenue that circulates throughout Christianity; one can easily be deceived by those things. As a result, many aspire to be prophets, and some place themselves in that role. They do not realize what they ask for and the destruction that comes with being in error. Let's explore this lesson in hopes that our senses will be sharpened to discern between the false and the true.

- How to know a false prophet. *Deuteronomy 18:20-22; Matthew 7:15-20.*
- The warning about false prophets. *Matthew 7:15; 24:24; II Corinthians 11: 11-15; II Peter 2:1.*
- Their punishment. *II Peter 2:4-9; Revelations 20:10.*
- Did the New Testament change the definition or role of the prophet?

Everyday Life Application

Name False prophets that were known to the world.

Speak of how their destruction came about.

Author: *Elder James Taylor, Jr.*

O THOU DECEITFUL TONGUE

Introduction

Our words are able to reach more people than ever before. Through the internet, your words can be broadcast live and heard around the world. As the popularity of podcasts and livestreams continue to increase, we must be aware of the implications of the words we speak. Whether our communication is daily talk at work or a worldwide broadcast; discretion is needed. The Bible provides warnings about the power of our words. "The tongue is a fire, a world of iniquity; so is the tongue among our members, that it defileth the whole body, and setteth on fire the course of nature; and it is set on fire of hell".

Memory Verse *Psalm 52:4* Thou lovest all devouring words, O thou deceitful tongue.

Biblical Application

Doeg the Edomite was the chiefest of the herdsmen that belonged to Saul. When Saul was trying to kill David, David stopped at Nob and came to Ahimelech the priest. Doeg was there and saw Ahimelech give David bread and a sword. Doeg later told Saul about David coming to Ahimelech. He lied and said that Ahimelech inquired of the Lord for David. His words began a course of events which resulted in the death of the Lord's priests. Let us be mindful of the words we speak; our words may have far greater implications than we realize.

- Doeg the Edomites words. *I Samuel 21:1-9, 22:6-23.*

- Doeg's tongue was like a sharp razor. *Psalm 52:1-5.*

- A world of iniquity. *James 3:1-12; Proverbs 12:17-19,22-23, 16:27-30, 18:4-8,13, 26:20-28; Leviticus 19:16.*

- Let thy words be few. *Ecclesiastes 5:1-3; Proverbs 10:18-21, 18:20-21; Ephesians 5:15-20.*

Everyday Life Application

What part does anger or other emotions play in the words we speak? How can hunger or lack of sleep influence the words you speak?

Lesson 40 July 17, 2021
Av 8, 5781

IS IT WISE TO OBEY?

Introduction

The wise man Solomon in *Proverbs 1:1-6*, says this of Wisdom: "To know wisdom and instruction; to perceive the words of understanding; To receive the instruction of wisdom, justice, and judgment, and equity; To give subtilty to the simple, to the young man knowledge and discretion. A wise man will hear, and will increase learning; and a man of understanding shall attain unto wise counsels: To understand a proverb, and the interpretation; the words of the wise, and their dark sayings." Proverbs is an insightful book on how to live our best life. It broadcasts the benefits of wisdom. Proverbs 9:10 states that the fear of the LORD is the beginning of wisdom: and the knowledge of the holy is understanding.

Memory Verse *Proverbs 2: 6* Then shalt thou understand the fear of the LORD, and find the knowledge of God.

Biblical Application

The Bible is full of accounts of man's failure to reach for wisdom in their approach to life's challenges. One such account is of Zedekiah, the king of Judah. Because of Judah's sins he was told by the Prophet Jeremiah to go with the king of Babylon into captivity. In this, God would preserve them and bring them again to their own Land (*Jeremiah 27*). The consequences for disobeying God's instructions would include his sons being killed in front of him, his eyes would be put out and many of the people would die. Wisdom says you would take God at his word. However, King Zedekiah listened to the words of false prophets like Hananiah (*Jeremiah 28*) which opened the door to tragedy rather than the door of life. (*Jeremiah 52*).

In addition, the Bible is full of accounts of man's insight to walk in wisdom. Such was the widow woman of Zarapeth *(I Kings 17: 8-16)* who in the time of the famine was making a cake for her and her son. She was doing this preparing to die. However, she was asked by the prophet Elijah to give him a drink and a cake, before she made one for her and her son. In doing so, by the word of the Lord the barrel of meal would not waste, neither would the cruse of oil fail, until the day that the LORD sends rain upon the earth. The widow woman went and did what Elijah said: and she, and he, and her house, ate for many days. The barrel of meal did not waste, neither did the cruse of oil fail, all according to the word of the LORD, which he spoke by Elijah. For today's lesson we pause for a moment to remind ourselves of the value in seeking wisdom.

Proverbs chapter 2, gives us a vivid picture to answer to the question of, wisdom? Why bother?

- How do we gain wisdom? *Proverbs 2:1-2.*
- What do you get when you seek her? *Proverbs 2: 4-10*
- Wisdom shows you the dangers *Proverbs 2: 11-22*

Everyday Life Application

There are many more Scriptures in *Proverbs* and in the *Bible* as a whole that announce the benefits of seeking and applying wisdom to your life journey, how many can you find?

Author: *Evangelist Patricia Powell*

TO SEEK AND TO SAVE

Introduction

Do you recall where you were when the Lord began to seek you? Did you recognize what was happening? At first, many of us resisted the call. Thankfully the Lord was merciful and longsuffering in seeking us. The Lord has loved us with an everlasting love; therefore, with lovingkindness he has drawn us. This is evident when Romans 5:8 declares, "But God commendeth his love toward us in that while we were yet sinners Christ died for us. . .". What did it take for you to reach the point of a broken spirit, a contrite heart to finally submit to God?

Memory Verse *Luke 19:10* For the Son of man is come to seek and to save that which was lost.

Biblical Application

Zacchaeus was a rich man and known as a chief publican. He desired to see Jesus among the multitude, but was short in stature. His curiosity caused him to run and climb a sycamore tree in order to get a glimpse of Jesus. Zacchaeus had a divine appointment to receive salvation. Jesus called him that day while he was in the tree and Zacchaeus received him joyfully. The Bible does not provide many details of what happened when Jesus came to his house. However; it does make it clear that during his time spent with the Messiah he came to a place of repentance. The message of the Messiah from the beginning of his ministry was: the time is fulfilled and the kingdom of God is at hand: repent ye, and believe the gospel. Jesus called many of us over and over before we finally submitted. The Lord is gracious and merciful in his desire to seek and save that which was lost. As we share the gospel message of repentance and faith in Jesus Christ, let us remember that no one is too far away for God to save. Salvation came to the house of a chief publican and sinner while the religious leaders murmured that Jesus was his guest. Let us be ambassadors for Christ endeavoring to reconcile the lost to Jesus.

- The message of Jesus. *Matthew 4:12-17; Luke 19:1-10, 9:51-56; Matthew 18:10-14.*
- As ambassadors we should be constrained by the love of Christ. *II Corinthians 5:14-21.*
- Let us not be like the religious leaders and hinder others. *Luke 11:45-54.*

Everyday Life Application

Have you ever been convicted by the Holy Spirit that you missed the opportunity to tell someone about Jesus during a one-time, unexpected encounter with an unknown person?

How can we maintain spiritual eyes to see all people as Christ does and be an effective witness?

THE INSEPARABLE CHRIST

Introduction

Inseparable is defined by Merriam Webster as: incapable of being separated or disjoined. Romans Chapter 8 discusses life through the Spirit. In this chapter, Paul stated that everyone who lives through Jesus Christ cannot be condemned because they are free from sin and death. The Apostle Paul begins by proclaiming that there is no condemnation for those who are in Christ Jesus. He ends the chapter assuring those in Christ that there is also no separation from the love of God. The phrase "love of Christ," as opposed to "love *for* Christ," refers to the love that He has toward mankind.

Memory Verse *Romans 8: 38-39* For I am persuaded, that neither death, nor life, nor angels, nor principalities, nor powers, nor things present, nor things to come, nor height, nor depth, nor any other creature, shall be able to separate us from the love of God, which is in Christ Jesus our Lord.

Biblical Application

According to Strong's Concordance, the word "persuaded" is the Greek word *peitho*. It means *to be convinced,* or *to be swayed from one opinion to the opinion held by another. Romans Chapter 8* declares that those who are with Christ are more than conquerors. Those who are with God should not fear anything else of the world because God is greater than all things. Scripture shows that Paul was at the height of his own excruciating trials, even at the very point of death, but he was fully persuaded of God's love for him. Paul uses the term "persuaded" in the sense of assurance. Paul's questions and answers in *Romans 8 verses 31-39* helps us when we: Are afraid (v.31); Are unsure that we can keep going as believers (v.32); feel guilty (vv.

33-34); and when we question or worry whether God loves us (vv.35-39). When Paul's questions are answered, the assurance issue is settled without a doubt. That in itself is a strong argument for assurance. This chapter convincingly shows that the believer is totally victorious. We are free from judgement because Christ died for us and we have His righteousness. We are free from defeat because Christ lives in us by His Spirit and we share His life. We are free from discouragement because Christ is coming for us and we will share His glory. We are free from fear because Christ intercedes for us and we cannot be separated from His love.

Believers are Constantly:

- Accompanied by His Presence. *Matthew 28:20*.

- Held close by His Hand. *John 10:28*.

- Like Branches in the Vine. *John 15:4*.

- In Perpetual Fellowship. John 17:23.

- No Power can dissever. Romans 8:38 – 8:39.

Everyday Life Application

Never forget the message Paul proclaimed. Nothing in this world has enough power to disconnect you from the love of God. If you've accepted Jesus Christ as Lord of your life, then you are inseparable from God's love.

Author: *Evangelist Irene Crawford*

DEAD TO SIN

Introduction

In time past we walked according to the course of this world, according to the prince of the power of the air, the spirit that now worketh in the children of disobedience. We all had our conversation in times past in the lusts of our flesh, fulfilling the desires of the flesh and mind. We were dead in our sins and the uncircumcision of our flesh. The Apostle Paul acknowledged that he was formerly a blasphemer, persecutor, and injurious, but did it ignorantly in unbelief. Some of us were dead in sin ignorantly while others practiced sin willfully. The Bible is clear we were dead in sin, but now we must be dead to sin.

Memory Verse *Romans 6:2* God forbid. How shall we that are dead to sin, live any longer therein?

Biblical Application

As baptized believers, we must reckon ourselves to be dead indeed unto sin. This includes making the choice to let not sin reign that we should obey it in the lusts thereof. Baptism is a beautiful natural picture of what occurs spiritually when we repent and come to Christ in faith for salvation. The Spirit of God performs a miracle in our lives that becomes evident naturally. We die spiritually with Christ and are buried with him in baptism into his death. Then just as Christ was raised from the dead, we are raised up with his resurrection power to walk in newness of life. Unfortunately, some people misunderstand water baptism as the means of salvation. Water baptism can be just another bath if the person has not truly repented of their sins and died to sin. For he that is dead is freed from sin; let us now yield ourselves to God as those that are alive from the dead.

- Water baptism is a natural picture of a spiritual event. *Romans 6: 1-14; Colossians 2: 6-15.*
- Depart from iniquity. *II Timothy 2:19-22; Psalm 19:12-14; I John 3: 2-10.*
- The old man is dead; do not resurrect him. *Isaiah 26:13-14;*
- *II Corinthians 5:17, 6:14-18, 1 Peter 2:24*

Everyday Life Application

What habits have you developed to overcome sin in your daily life?

Have the people you associated with or places you visited ever influenced you to sin?

Does Satan have as much power to influence you to sin as many people claim?

FORNICATION

Introduction

Paul warned about the pitfalls of the "flesh". The flesh is basically the part of us that has not responded to God and lives by its own desires. These desires are incredibly strong and can have destructive natural consequences. Cravings creep up on us and we find ourselves in trouble with God and our community. One of the more prominent results of being led by the flesh is the unlawful sexual relationships that take place outside of marriage. Fornication must be seen as a shameful act and that narrative must not change. This subject has been shrouded in shame, but we have the power to change the narrative on this important topic of life.

Memory Verse *I Corinthians 6:18* Flee fornication. Every sin that a man doeth is without the body; but he that committeth fornication sinneth against his own body.

Biblical Application

Fornication is not a problem associated with the youth only; it is a human problem. We must take the opportunity to teach the proper dynamics for sexual and intimate relationships. These relationships are divine and we can learn about them from God through His Word. The correct type of intimate relationship will only enhance our lives.

- Fornication is a selfish act, proof of immaturity, and operating out of God's design. I Cor 6:9-20
- Paul talked about one avenue for defeating fornication, marriage. I Cor 7:1-40

- There is beauty in committed, exclusive relationships that deepen intimacy. Song of Solomon 7:1-13
- You control your body and who it is shared with. Col 3:5

Everyday Life Application

Fornication is a choice. You choose to go against God with that choice. Choose wisely with your vessel. Consequences of sex outside of marriage range from sexually transmitted diseases, emotional destruction, unplanned pregnancy, and addiction. It is an enemy that can be defeated.

Author: *Elder David T. Brand Jr. MA, LPC*

WHEN THOU DOEST ALMS

Introduction

Psalms 24:1 "The earth is the Lord's and the fullness thereof; the world, and they that dwell therein". The Lord has allowed us to be stewards over that which belongs to Him. We are able participate in his providing for others through that with which He has entrusted to us. Scripture gives examples of God providing for others through people. Specific instructions are also given regarding our willingness to give.

Memory Verse *Matthew 6:3* But when thou doest alms, let not thy left hand know what thy right hand doeth.

Biblical Application

When the land and vineyards were harvested, the Lord commanded not to wholly reap the corners nor gather every grape. These were to be left to the poor and to the stranger. The Lord told Moses to take offerings for the tabernacle of every man that giveth it willingly. It is more blessed to give than to receive; God loves a cheerful giver. The Bible is clear that we are to do alms or benefaction toward the poor (Strong's Dictionary). Jesus talked about hypocrites who did alms with the wrong motivation; they sounded the trumpets to be seen of and receive glory of men. Unfortunately, this is similar to some practices used in offerings today. Special recognition is offered for the amount of money given in offerings and places in prayer lines are even designated on the amount of money given. Let us examine the Scriptures regarding giving.

- Consider the poor, strangers, fatherless, and widows. *Leviticus 19: 9-10; Deuteronomy 24:19-22, 15:7-11; Psalm 112:5,9; Proverbs 19:17.*

- When thou doest alms. *Matthew 6:1-4.*

- Give with a willing heart. *Exodus 25: 2, 35:5, 21; Leviticus 1: 1-3; II Corinthians 9:1-11; Luke 6:38.*
- Beware of covetousness. *Luke 12:13-34.*

Everyday Life Application

How can you practice wisdom in giving to the homeless? Why did God say to bring the tithes and offerings into the storehouse?

JESUS, HEALER

Introduction

The word "heal" and "healing" means to make solid or whole. It is defined as the process of making or becoming sound or healthy again. In the Bible it means the restoration of health, the making whole or well whether physically, mentally or spiritually. In the Old Testament the LORD God (Yahweh) alone was the source of all healing. The Bible shows the positive role of physicians and medicines. Physicians were needed in biblical times as they are needed now. Obviously, they had limited knowledge, but the knowledge they had acquired was applied. The following scriptures shows that there was knowledge and use of medicine and physicians without condemnation. See *Genesis 15:2; II Chronicles 16:12; Job 13:4; and Jeremiah 8:22* for some Old Testament examples. No Scripture condemns the legitimate use of doctors or medical science. In the New Testament, there are various references made by Jesus to medicines and medical assistance (*Luke 10:25-37*). One such example is found in Luke 5:31, when Jesus in making a point, compared physical and spiritual healing, he said; "...they that are whole need not a physician; but they that are sick."

Memory Verse *Exodus 15:26* ". . .and said, if thou wilt diligently hearken to the voice of the LORD thy God, and wilt do that which is right in his sight, and wilt give ear to his commandments, and keep all his statutes, I will put none of these diseases upon thee, which I have brought upon the Egyptians: for I am the LORD that healeth thee".

Biblical Application

Scripture teaches that God has power and authority over all disease, famine, peril and sickness. Jesus Christ is the Master Healer and He has a plan to bring healing to your life. A great portion of Christ's time was dedicated to healing the sick and downtrodden. He healed all kinds of people, including the blind, the paralyzed, the deaf, the lame, lepers, those who had fever, and many with chronic illnesses. There is no record in the Gospels of Jesus turning away anyone who came to Him for healing. We also know from Scripture that there was no sickness or disease that was too difficult for Him to heal. Jesus healed "every disease and sickness among the people" in Galilee (*Matthew 4:23*), Judea (Matthew 19:1-2), and everywhere He went (*Mark 6:56*) to authenticate His Messiahship (*John 7:31*).

According to Scriptures, the Father has the power to heal the whole person.

- Spiritually. *Psalm 103:2-3; Jeremiah 3:22; I Peter 2:24; Isaiah 53:5.*
- Physically. *II Kings 5:10; Isaiah 38:15-16; Psalm 41:3, 107:19-20; Matthew 14:14.*
- Emotionally. *Psalm 34:18, Psalm 147:3.*
- Mentally. *Daniel 4:31-34.*

Everyday Life Application

Remember and discuss various miraculous things that cannot be explained without attributing it to the healing power of Jesus.

Source: https://www.christianity.com/wiki/christian-life/what-does-the-bible-say-about-healing.html

Author: *Evangelist Irene Crawford*

GUARD AGAINST FALSE TEACHING

Introduction

In America alone, there are thousands of denominations and hundreds of thousands of churches. There are gospel programs on radio and T.V. that have material 24 hours a day and 7 days a week. There are many of these churches and denominations teaching information contrary to the word of God, and often times leading people astray. Though it's a sad thing to see, it's no surprise. For Satan has always manipulated Scripture and been very subtle in applying his agenda (*Matthew 4:6*), thus we as believer's, have to be mindful of the info that's being delivered.

Memory Verse *Isaiah 5:20* Woe unto them that call evil good, and good evil; that put darkness for light, and light for darkness; that put bitter for sweet, and sweet for bitter?

Biblical Application

The Bible throughout its entirety speaks out against false teaching. The Word of God is of the utmost importance. For this reason, we must always be on guard. For it is that; a guide to every aspect of our lives. His Word keeps us aligned with his perfect will. To combat false teaching, believer's, must spend time reading and studying the word. It is also important to understand context, and not isolate a particular verse, but to allow Scripture to define Scripture; for the Bible will not contradict itself.

- Importance of the Whole Bible. *II Timothy 3:16-17; Matthew 5:18.*
- Warnings against false teaching. *Hebrew 13:9; II Peter 2:1-11.*

- Don't give heed to them. *I Timothy 1: 3-4; II Timothy 2:16-18.*
- How to combat false teaching. *II Timothy 2:15; Isaiah 28: 9-10.*
- God's attitude about his Word. *Matthew 5:19; Revelation 22: 18-19.*

Everyday Life Application

Can you name some of the false doctrines being taught?

Name some doctrines that are true, but are being taught out of balance?

Author: *Elder James Taylor, Jr.*